DEARLY loved EXILE

By Janell Mellish

unfailing Loves
Never Shaken

Janell

ISBN: 978-0-692-84354-3

Cover Design: Chiara Pennella

Edited by: Patricia Green

Published by: RWB Publishing

Also available in ebook publication

PRINTED IN THE UNITED STATES OF AMERICA

Dearly Loved Exile
A Journey to Find the Temple of the Most High
By Janell Mellish

Personal accounts throughout, are used with permission.

Contents

DEDICATION

This book is dedicated to

Charleigh Nicole Mellish

"All God's grace in one little face"

ABOUT DEARLY LOVED EXILE

As a new day dawns, there remains an underlying truth for each of us to reconcile. Each of us faces the chance to doing everything by our own power, exactly right. We face the chance to find ourselves in the middle of tragedy, heartbreak and on occasion, stuck right in the epicenter of our own worst nightmare. Our world changes from a life of freedom to a life of captivity within our own soul in a mere instant. Not everyone understands what this looks like, but we all face the possibility that it could be us next time. Next time could be your time.

In this heart wrenching chronicle, the author shares her experience of finding her own soul after walking through tragedy. The hope she found was buried deep in the Old Testament of the Bible. The Old Testament is a portion of the Bible that is often overlooked, yet walks us through the turmoil, heartbreak and devastation the Israelite's experienced as they watched their beloved temple ravaged. Their future was to become enslaved as a group of broken exiles. A covenant with God meant meeting with Him in the temple, but it lay in ruin. It is through their 70 years of captivity and heartbreak that their level of devotion grew to a God that loved them beyond any earthly measure. A new sense of devotion and understanding emerged out of their disaster. That beautifully orchestrated, divine plan of provisions is the same truth the author discovered through her journey.

Janell will warm your heart no matter what season you are in as she walks you through the words of the Bible that bring hope, confidence, and an understanding to a love incomparable to anything you have ever known. She may not answer your questions of *why*, but she will reassure you that in the midst of the darkness there is a light that is waiting to reach into your soul and fill it with the beauty of the temple. Your heart is what God longs for. He has proven His dedication to you before. If you can find the courage to allow Him to fight for you while in your heartbreak, you will be amazed by His goodness, grace, and His unfailing love.

The Israelites remembered their temple. They remembered the beauty of what once was and they mourned their loss. A future without the temple seemed a wasteland. As we watch our own lives and everything we valiantly built in those lives fall apart; we remember. We remember our innocence that is lost. The only future possibility that stands confirmed is that there is absolutely no going back. As we genuinely offer our hearts to God, our exiled hearts begin to treasure once was and we find new hope for an even more loved and cherished future. Our temples begin to resemble more of a pleasant offering to God as our dedication grows and a sincere beauty emerges. This is the journey of the exile to find the temple.

You are the temple, ***dearly loved exile***!

ADVANCE PRAISE FOR
DEARLY LOVED EXILE

In *Dearly Loved Exile*, a deeply personal acknowledgement of tragedy, Janell Mellish leads us on a journey toward embracing our captivity and brokenness. Most of us want to run away, hide, and find fault or justification in our circumstances. Janell help us see God's purpose in all of it, and how He guides, not around the pain but through it. The book is inspirational and a true gift from God.

Shawna D.

I recently had the privilege of reading *Dearly Loved Exile*. I am honored that my feedback was solicited for this book. I believe the strongest part of the book for me was the way the author paralleled her own healing/rebuilding after tragedy with the Israelites healing and rebuilding. It allowed me to look at that period of history for the Jews in a different light and it was very helpful, beneficial for me. A few other things I liked were the author's honesty, the use of Scripture and her vulnerability.

Laura W.

The book was amazing. I knew Janell and her family for a short time, she has a heart to minister to ALL. I believe this book will touch many lives who are hurt, broken, and worn out from circumstances they can't seem to get over. How she exposed her heart and her emotions are really remarkable. It takes a lot of guts to put it out there for the whole world to see. I have already recommended this book to a friend whose husband committed suicide, and she found him.

Pastor JT

I like the weaving in and out of the two stories of captivity. There are many great insights. Janell is allowing others to benefit from her deepest pain, something most people hesitate to do.

Miriam C

I enjoyed the book and found the concept of looking at ourselves as Temples to be a different insight and also very powerful. There were a lot of things discussed in the Old Testament that were presented in a new and different way.

Brandon A.

Dearly Loved Exile is a must read! In a place of devastation, how does a soul find healing? How does a person reconcile a God who loves and a life that is broken? Janell gives a voice to the crushed soul and hope to the broken because… She has been there! Not only has she been there but she has also gone through the wilderness and is speaking from a place of victory! Her words strengthen the heart and call out to join herin what can be! Following God is rarely easy and pain is a part of the journey. But take heart, Dearly Loved Exile, reminds us that though we may feel exiled… the truth is, we are dearly loved!

Pastor KW

This book is a biblically sound book that lays out a practical way of turning Tragedy into Triumphant. It will bring you face to face with the hurts of life and reveal how to turn it into a victory of celebration of joy. Janell, shares her personal walk with God and how she and God got through such a great and difficult experience. I highly recommend it to all who have experienced a great tragedy in life, you will find a welcome friend as you read this book. And thank you Janell to be willing to open your wounds to share in your victory, God Bless this book!

Pastor John M.

FOREWORD

There are moments in each person's life that alter the course of our life *forever*, and then there are the moments that change *us* forever.

Several years ago, I was blessed to have one of those *forever* moments when I met Janell Mellish.

I was standing in the lobby of a church when Janell walked over and we talked about the women's boxing gym that she had recently opened in Cheyenne, Wyoming called *Pink Gloves Boxing*. She shared her warrior's heart, drawing me into a conversation about how any workout can alter not only the figure but also the outlook and the *life* of the participant.

Janell is passionate about her love for God, her husband, and her two children. She is passionate about helping others to reach their full potential. This passion was tested to the limits, however, on a very ordinary morning when she was confronted with a moment that changed her *forever*.

A man stepped in front of her car on a major interstate in San Antonio and was killed. In that moment, her life, as she knew it, was also killed.

Dearly Loved Exile is Janell's walk through that *forever* moment. We accompany her and glimpse the injuries, setbacks, and heartaches that she experienced. Nothing could have prepared me for the visceral reaction I had to the pain and truths she reveals in her book.

As with all things that have God's hand on them, the rays of light begin to shine again, and Janell starts the arduous task of rebuilding her life. First one stone and then another, and soon a Holy foundation is laid, and a temple of God's making rises again, more beautiful than ever before.

Brad Enzi

Founder Leadership 3D

PART ONE

CHAPTER ONE

YOU

The Temple of the Most High

The most beautiful place on earth is highly debatable. Some would likely argue it is somewhere in the Caribbean ocean, with the crystal clear blue waters. Others might conclude that the most beautiful place is the Grand Canyon, where you can witness the results of the mighty hand of God. Or, maybe some would argue that it is Yellowstone National Park, amid wild animals that give evidence of the things God created in Genesis. Perhaps an ocean view with a spectacular sunset, or the enormous hills found through the peaceful Rocky Mountains with nothing else to quite compare to the grandiosity. Although these are some of my personal favorite places to witness how big our God is, they still lack something. God's Word tells me exactly the reason for this lack of ultimate fulfillment.

When God created all these things in Genesis, He saw that it was *good*. But then in Genesis 2:31, after creating man, He saw that it was *very good*. Places on earth witness about God, but people are His *reflection*. This explains why *I* would argue that the most fulfilling, awe inspiring, beautiful place I have ever been is with my grandparents. There seems to be a greater reflection of God shining brighter here than anywhere else. They understand life beyond anything else on earth. They have seen the atrocities of war, rebuilding of economies, the death of loved ones, burying of spouses, heartache incomparable to what I can't even imagine, the beauty of a grandchild and so many other experiences that have built in them character that no book or school could teach. This knowledge is just a small reflection of God, yet it shines brighter than anything else on earth.

Recently, I stood beside my husband's grandmother as she said her goodbyes to her husband of 68 years. As he hung on to those last, precious moments, she spoke the words that every wife dreads to the man she loves. God designed the husband to be the head of the household, but there comes a time for some wives to let their leader go. As our dear grandmother encouraged him to run into the loving arms of his maker, she did it without breaking down. Somehow, her small 86-year-old body reflected a courage and strength that transcends human strength and understanding. Her beauty was more apparent than ever in those moments. In my eyes, she became the most beautiful woman I had ever seen. Through her, there was an enormous amount of love that filled the room, as a reflection of God's love. She became a living reflection of Jesus's sacrificial, unselfish love. This supernatural love she demonstrated proves we have a God. It proves that we were never designed to live on our terms, or according to our own strength. At that moment, I realized that we truly can do all things through Christ, who gives us strength.

Grandpa's last words came from a divine strength as well. His concern was not for himself, but for his wife, and to make sure his Easter offering was taken care of (and to make it a little extra this year). His love for his wife and for God's mission on this earth was greater than any selfish concern over the fear of death. Although his body was failing and his appearance weak, his beauty was greater than ever. *This* type of beauty surpasses anything this world could offer or give.

We spend our lifetimes building our character, whether intentional or not. Every lesson, each failure, every memory is used to build this body, mind, and spirit. We take the steps necessary to grow into people who have a more advanced understanding of this world just through experience. The deep creases and lines on our face and, perhaps for some of us, a head lacking the hair it once had, have a deeper meaning behind it. Perhaps it reflects heartbreak, or a sleepless night watching a precious newborn staring innocently back at you, or a tiresome week spent in a hospital watching a loved one fighting to live, or perhaps a knock on the door that changes your life. This *shell* that we see staring back at us in the mirror is what God said was *very good*. At some point, instead of staring back at the reflection with pride we tend to look with a quick glimpse simply because we must. Somewhere along the way, we forget to appreciate the road we have walked. Why do we struggle to accept ourselves as what God made wasn't only good, but *very* good?

The apostle Paul asked each of us in 1 Corinthians 3:16, "Don't you know that you yourselves are God's temple and that God's Spirit lives in you"? Again in 1 Corinthians 6:19, "Do you not know that your body is a temple of the Holy Spirit, who is in you, whom you received from God?". This word *temple* (Greek translation of *naos*) is the same word Jesus used when He was questioned by the Jews. They wanted to know what authority He had to demand them to stop exploiting each other under the name of proper worship in the "Naos, the temple." He responds to their question in John 2:19 by saying:

> *"Destroy this temple, and I will raise it again in three days. The Jews replied, "It has taken forty-six years to build this temple and you are*

*going to raise it in three days? But the <u>temple</u>
he had spoken of was his body."*

The same word "Naos" is used after Christ died
on the cross in Mathew 27:51 (Mark 15:38, Luke
23:45). The verse(s) say that after Jesus had taken his
last breath, the "curtain of the *temple* was torn in two
from top to bottom." Do you see a connection yet?

If we are a *temple,* then it's important to stop
for a second and distinguish the difference between a
temple and a *building.* When Paul asked the people if
they knew they were a temple, it meant something
more in that day than it would to us today. I believe
we often mistake this to mean simply *a pretty
important building.* However, typically when we talk
about a building, we are merely talking about a hard
shell of materials used to enclose an area to be used as
protection from the elements. <u>In the Old Testament, a
temple was a unique building containing a Holy place
and the Holy of Holies.</u> This is the place where the
image of God dwelled in the Old Testament! This is
also referred to as the "divine dwelling place and the

place of divine manifestation" by Helps-Word Studies. Strong's Concordance refers to this part of the "temple where God himself resides." We don't have buildings like this today. Is it possible that we miss the true meaning when Paul tells us (believers) that *we* are the temples?

So, we must ask ourselves again, do you see yourself as a temple? Not just as a shell, but a place where the Creator of Heaven and Earth dwells? A place in which *El Elyon* (The Most High God), *El Olam* (The Everlasting God), *Jehovah Jireh* (The Lord Will Provide), *Jehovah Shalom* (The Lord is Peace) resides? Is this the place that *Jehovah Shammah* (The Lord is There) can be found?

When we base our worth on who *we* think we are, chances are most of us will lean towards an *unsatisfactory* rating. I'm not a believer of *magic*, but a magical thing happens to my soul when I think of myself not as a sinner who is always struggling, but as a temple of Adonai (My Lord, My Master). This body that typically feels like an empty shell suddenly becomes a living, breathing, reflection of our God. We begin to grasp the fact that we were created in the image of God. This changes everything about what we do, how we treat ourselves, what we choose to do with our time...those mundane minutes become precious moments to draw closer to our God, to get a taste of our eternity as we serve Him wholeheartedly.

Is it no wonder why the Apostle Paul asked the question twice within several chapters, "Do you know your body is a temple of God?" I imagine if Paul roamed this earth today, and we brought our problems to him, his response would again be that question. As we devalue ourselves and struggle with addictions, sinful activities and unhealthy pursuits, I see Paul asking, "Don't you know...?" with a confused look on his face. I can imagine myself explaining to Paul how unsatisfied I am with my body. I would sound like a broken record player going through all that I'm not without even allowing him a moment to ask if I realize that I am more than just that. Well, don't we know?

Leaning on our own understanding of who we are, mere survival will be a challenge. Without understanding our purpose on this earth, we are left without hope. We become lost in a selfish pursuit of finding the worldly promise of happiness that leads to chasing our own tails. If you let the world speak its *truth* into you, you are setting yourself up for a fall. If you rely on the worth that the appearance of your body will bring, prepare for disaster. Wouldn't it be great if someone could convince your mind that your value is much higher than what you tend to believe?

On a recent trip from Salt Lake City, Utah to Great Falls, Montana during a cold February day I happened to notice the beatings that the concrete barriers through Salt Lake City took. You can see the black tire marks from where vehicles have made contact. Some tire marks appear to have left the ground to touch a part of the barrier. That seems to be impossible if the vehicle was traveling in the designed manner. About the time you forget about the evidence from an obvious horrible accident, you come upon another set of reminders something horrible happened at a different location. This is the view repeatedly throughout the hour-long trek on I-15 through the Salt Lake area.

If I could see the evidence of my own past, would it show the same evidence as the carnage on the interstate? How about you? There have been times that my heart felt comparable to the carnage left on the wall. Would your track record be similar?

Most likely, a good portion of these vehicles that hit the concrete barriers paid the price for someone else's misfortune, bad driving or simple lack of paying attention. Through no fault of their own, they paid for being in the wrong place at the wrong time.

We can assume one fact from the evidence left behind. At some point, these vehicles had some sort of help. People arrived to help them clean the mess, get medical attention and figure out how to move on. I know this to be true because there are no vehicles on the side of the road, nor any people sitting waiting for medical help, nor any other evidence that there was an accident there.

At some point, every accident was cleaned up. We can assume that some took longer than others. All that is left to testify of the accident are the marks left on the barrier. We can also deduce from the evidence, some accidents were worse than others. Some can make you cringe thinking of what a vehicle had to do to make those kinds of marks.

If you don't believe me, look at the concrete barriers next time you drive through a city. Pick any of them, and you will see the same evidence.

On that February day, as I drove through Utah, Idaho and finally Montana the weather continued to get worse and colder. By the time I was within an hour of Great Falls, I had come upon a single vehicle accident. Despite the weather, the roads were clear until you came to the point that the road circled around a great valley that follows the Missouri River. I was traveling along at 75 miles per hour and came upon a huge curve. As you entered the curve the road was completely clear, but as you turned the road became progressively icier until the road was completely covered with snow and ice. A truck that was probably a half hour ahead of me had probably thought the curve would be clear and so didn't see a need to slow down. The same thoughts I had as I made the turn, but as he rounded the corner, went into an inevitable slide that sent him straight into the concrete median.

Comparatively, many of our knocks come from a slow slide that sin sends us into. By the time we recognize what is happening, we are already feeling the collision.

Lucky for me, by the time I came upon the spot of the accident the First Responders were already there, slowing travelers down and warning drivers of the threat. As I rounded the turn and witnessed the smashed truck at the barrier, I was overly grateful for the warning.

How often this happens in our own lives. We are warned of danger, and sometimes we heed, while other times we don't slow down and around the next turn we learn the hard way. It makes me think that maybe my life really is "a Highway," like Tom Cochran sings about. A song, once an adult hit, became popular to little boys and girls around the world through the cartoon "Cars," sung by Rascal Flatts. Particularly the part that says "Knock me down, get back up again," but a life with Jesus is why we can agree with the part that says,

> *"There ain't no load that I can't hold*
> *Road so rough this I know*
> *I'll be there when the light comes in*
> *Just tell 'em we're survivors"*

I love traveling some of the country back roads in Montana and Wyoming seeing some of the old, abandoned farm houses, churches, and schools. It makes my mind wonder what used to be there. I can imagine the kids sitting in an old-school house, or the families working in the old barns. In the same manner, I have looked at myself in the mirror and remembered what used to be. Like many of you, I've wondered what will come when the innocence is lost. Being beat down by the world can lead to feeling like an old shack that used to be something beautiful. The innocence and simplicity of life seem to be gone.

There is an important distinction that must be made between a building and a temple. For the

Israelites in the Old Testament, the structure of a temple wasn't what made it valuable. It wasn't merely a building that they enjoyed being in. The difference was what dwelled inside those four walls of the temple; the presence of God. That mere fact made it critical to rebuilding the temple.

Often, we view ourselves as merely a structure. We would likely agree that our bodies are essential for survival. We all know that we need to take care of it to live long, healthy lives. However, when we allow ourselves to be continually beaten down and trampled by sin or by others, that may be symptomatic of viewing ourselves as a building instead of a temple. Many of us would agree and describe ourselves as resembling an old, abandoned house. That isn't what Paul told us we are. That isn't how God views us either. So, why it is that we allow the world to dictate our importance?

Happily-ever-after tales are hard for a lot of us to relate to. Our life often resembles something very different, leaving us jaded at the mere idea of a *happily-ever-after*. Unfortunately, the Guide to life (the Bible) never says *happily-ever-after* either. I firmly believe the greatest lessons learned are those hard ones that we must struggle through.

The words that are laid out in front of you wouldn't be attractive to those who lead perfect, comfortable, unchallenged lives. Which begs to answer the question, does that even exist? I've recently met a group of people that spent all their time trying to convince each other of their perfect lives. Yet, when looking at the whole picture, it was obvious things weren't perfect. My life and openness about it absolutely freaked them out. In fact, the word they used for where I need to be to minister to others is in a *clinic*. As I've met more and more people along my path, I've realized that the world I walk in is a clinic of many broken hearts. For those people, often until their brokenness reaches a level deeper than the need for perfection, they will refuse to acknowledge anything different. On the contrary to allowing ourselves to become abandoned houses when Paul tells us we are temples, he doesn't mean that we will be perfect either.

As we face the trials of our life, we long to have a story that we can relate to. We often look for someone else's story to bring us hope. We want to know that there is a light at the end of the tunnel. We want evidence to reassure us that God will bring us through. We want outlined steps to direct us how to get there.

It should be of no surprise that tucked in the middle of the Old Testament, we find such a story. Would you be surprised to hear that it is the beautiful story of the building, destruction, and rebuilding of the Temple? This story shines a light on how we can build ourselves to withstand the beatings of this world.

Here's my disclaimer. This story isn't a story without heartbreak. You will witness victory and beauty, and then you will see that all torn down. For this story to take root in your soul, you must remember that this is more than a fictional story. This is a real story. Not only is it true, but it is also part of our story. It is our story of why we can live in the freedom that we have. This story explains why we live differently from those who don't know our merciful, loving, and all-knowing, all-seeing Creator.

Perhaps you are reading this and do not believe in the Bible. My hope and prayer are that you may put this to the test.

This story, I have found, brings us hope that is incomparable to anything that this earth can offer. Not only does it offer hope, but also an example of courage to face the struggles and hardships of this world.

So many books and expert advice is centered on living a happy life, being the best you, and ultimate success. They lead us to believe that we can accomplish all that using our own will power. Unfortunately, we try this every day and discover that it's just not how the world we live in works. We are never promised these qualities in describing our life. We are left to search for the strength to be the light of the world amongst the darkness. Through this journey something beautiful happens, we begin to discover a deeper meaning and purpose in this world.

Some people, even other Christ followers, will read that paragraph and not understand what I am speaking of. I can't explain that. I don't know why some of us struggle so hard, while others skip through this life. These are usually the people that say things like, "can't you just get over it?" or "one of these days you will forget about your struggle and focus on better things" or "just hand it over to God, what's the problem." The ignorance of some Christians is disheartening for me, and yet I still can't explain it.

Christians can be shallow, naïve, judgmental and very hurtful to those amid struggle. Ultimately, this judgmental attitude reflects horribly upon the Christian faith to those standing on the outside.

If we were to view each other as the *temples* that we are to God, we would be more willing to walk through the fire with one another. We would love each other more, forgive easier, and be more strongly connected through the spirit. And yet, what we normally do is try to *fix* each other.

There was a period of my life that people either had all the wrong answers for me or they avoided me because of the circumstances of my life. It explains why we have a saying that we often use during a crisis, that goes like this, "you'll find out who you real friends are." We say that because it holds so much truth. Social media reinforces this day after day to me.

This morning I saw a picture on Facebook of a horse stuck in mud up to its chest, exhausted from trying to get out it couldn't hold its head up, so a lady had jumped in and was holding it for the horse until help arrived. This picture makes headlines because it doesn't happen every day that someone would jump into the mud and keep a head above the mud. Yet this is precisely what a good friend will do. They will jump in with us and help hold us up until we get our strength back. We all know that it isn't a fun or easy path by any means. When we walk it, we discover that it is a path with meaning. Only God can give us the strength to walk that path.

A pastor, whom I deeply admire, said in one of his latest sermons that "my job is not to coddle you but to help push you into the truth. You can lead a horse to water, but you can't make him drink, but I sure can hold your head under the water until you change your mind." While I know he wasn't being literal, I loved that he was willing to step outside of his comfort zone to help someone else. Loving each other in this way is the hard way. This is the way that Jesus would have responded. Instead, out of our own discomfort, we often respond by turning a blind eye.

There's a short story in the Bible that speaks of how Jesus stepped out to help others. This story is found in three books of the gospel (Matthew 12, Mark 3, and Luke 6). It is a story about a man with a shriveled hand. All three accounts point out that the Pharisees were watching Jesus to see if He would heal this man on the Sabbath. If Jesus did heal the man, it would give them a reason to accuse Jesus of a crime. Luke 8:8 tells us that Jesus knew what their intentions were before He did anything. To heal this man would mean giving these people a reason to plot to kill Him. Not helping this man would be the safe and easy way out for Jesus. Many of us today would likely pretend not to see the man out of our own selfishness. Instead, Jesus responds with this:

"If any of you has a sheep and it falls into a pit on the Sabbath, will you not take hold of it and lift it out? How much more valuable is a man than a sheep! Therefore it is lawful to do good on the Sabbath" Matthew 12:11-12

Jesus was making a point here about the Sabbath, but helping this man cost Him something, and it isn't just a little something. In all three accounts, the story ends by telling us that the Pharisees leave to plot to *kill* Him. Jesus was telling us that helping others is worth the cost. Not just on the Sabbath, but every single day, every single time. Those around Jesus were focused on all the wrong things. It was easier to judge Jesus than it was to deal with a man with a shriveled hand.

Jesus saw a temple. They saw a shriveled hand. The account in Mark tells us how Jesus responded to their misdirected attention:

"He looked around at them in anger and, deeply distressed at their stubborn hearts, said

to the man, "stretch out your hand."" Mark
3:5

That word *distressed* is translated in other
translations of the Bible that Jesus was *deeply
saddened* and *grieved*. Strong's Concordance gives
the definition of "being moved to grief by sympathy."
Can you imagine Jesus looking around Him and seeing
the judgmental, disapproving faces around Him and
being moved and deeply saddened?

I can imagine this. I know you can too. We
have all seen it. I've experienced looking around me in
my brokenness to perceive only judgment towards my
lack of perfection at that moment. I must admit that I
have likely been on the other end of it as well.

The point is that we can't allow others around
us to convince us that we aren't worthy of help, or that
our shriveled hand isn't a problem in the first place. So
many people walk around with a shriveled-up body
(temple) lacking the spiritual nutrients needed to be
healthy, yet claim to be *completely holy*, *perfect*, and
sin free. We are instructed by the living Word of God

to deal with our problems. Take your shriveled hand to Jesus and find those spirit-fed friends that will jump in the mud to love you through it.

The story about the temple will help us learn to unveil our brokenness to the One Healer who can heal it. We will be privileged as we witness the character of God unveiled. We will see the steps to rebuild a broken soul. A temple will be rebuilt. We will understand the purpose of being rebuilt is that there may be light amid a broken world. There is a purpose for each of us, and time in this world to fulfill the great commission, so instead of fighting the pain, let's see it rebuilt.

Let's ask the question once more before we let God convince us of the Truth, "Don't you know that you are a temple?"

CHAPTER TWO

A TEMPLE BUILT BY A DIVINE DESIGN

The Desert Tabernacle

I often wonder if the Israelites knew just how amazing the tabernacle was. Were they able to grasp the majestic beauty of it? They couldn't have possibly understood the incredible story God was creating amidst their journey.

In the first four books of the Bible, we discover Moses' incredible trek through the desert. This journey began after God freed the Israelite people from the harsh slavery of the Egyptian Pharaoh. Through trials and tribulations, God brought the people through the desert after 40 years. At the end of those 40 years, they are delivered directly to the land that had been promised to the generations before them.

If you have ever read Exodus, you'll remember that a huge portion of the chapter is about the detailed instructions on how the Israelite people were to build their tabernacle. It was in this tabernacle that God would dwell with them. His Holy presence filled the tabernacle. When it was time for the Israelites to move, God would lead them with a cloud and fire. During the day a cloud would rise above the tabernacle, and at night a fire would rise above it. These elements would guide the people in the direction that God wanted them to go.

The story of the Israelites wandering in the desert is such an incredible story from start to finish. If you aren't familiar or maybe haven't read the story in a while, let me give you a quick reminder.

It all begins with an Israelite baby. In the time of this baby boy's birth, the Egyptian Pharaoh demanded that all the Israelite baby boys be killed. This baby named Moses should have been killed. Instead, he was hidden in a basket, floated down the river and found by none other than the Pharaoh's daughter. She adopted Moses, and he grew up in

Pharaoh's house. Moses began to understand his situation and what his true heritage was as an Israelite. He witnessed the harsh treatment of his people by the Egyptians and eventually took matters into his own hands. In a moment of rage, he killed an Egyptian guard who was beating one of his people. Instead of thanking him, his people turned against him and sent him fleeing the country. This story, however, is far from over.

God eventually responds to the cries of anguish from the Israelite people. He calls Moses to lead them to freedom. At the time, Moses was 40 years old and so broken he questioned God. God appeared to Moses as a burning bush and yet Moses still questioned God. Moses used every excuse that we still use today as to why he couldn't lead God's people. You know, all the typical excuses like "I can't," "It's too hard," and "I don't know how." Isn't it interesting how we claim to trust God to know more than we know, but when He calls us, we doubt the calling? We doubt our capabilities when it isn't our abilities that we rely on, but His.

God reassured Moses in every one of his doubts. So, Moses went back to a land that he once fled. Through God's provisions and strength, Moses demanded that the Pharaoh let the Israelite people go. Unfortunately, Pharaoh's heart was so hardened to God that he denied letting the people go. He continued to make the Israelites lives harder. God sent nine plagues to convince the Pharaoh. The Pharaoh continually rejected God, until finally, God sent the Passover. It was the night that every first-born son was killed except the ones who had the blood of the lamb on the doorposts that got Pharaoh's attention. He finally released God's people. God provided some impressive miracles as the Israelite people left. The parting of the Red Sea is probably the most told. It's an amazing story of how God provided and continually protected his beloved. However, it's frustrating to see how disobedient and distrusting these people were to such an amazing God.

A beautiful agreement was made between God and His chosen people. This promise is referred to as "The Covenant." Moses received guidance that he shared with the people, and if they would follow these, then God would give them possession of the land that had been promised (Dt. 4:1). In fact, God promised that they would become His *treasured possession*, and a holy nation if they would follow his instructions (Exodus 19:5-6). The laws that Moses told the people are hints to God's character for us and reflect mercy and grace, which was something unfamiliar to the Israelites. What a great deal offered to the Israelites. As Moses presented the deal to the Israelites, they answered with a binding statement of "We will" (verse 8). They promised to do *everything* that the Lord told them. With the *we will*, they acknowledged that they trusted God. They testify to believe what God said was true and that they would lean not on their own understanding, but on what the Divine plan was. Would you be surprised to hear that their faith lacked in the same ways we struggle today?

This covenant was based on the Israelites sacrifices and offerings to God to receive forgiveness. Remember, this was before Jesus' time. Their sacrifices weren't a one-time requirement, but a routine obligation to receive forgiveness. To offer their sacrifices, they were directed to build an altar of *burnt offering*. The altar was made of acacia wood and overlaid with bronze with horns on each corner of the altar to secure the sacrifice. Moses didn't think of this system by himself but was given detailed instructions by God. God reminds Moses that all this was to be done exactly as he had instructed.

This altar was placed at the entrance of the temple and offerings were made twice a day. It was through the blood of the lambs sacrificed that God could forgive his people. Forgiveness was a necessity so that God could "meet with the Israelites, and the place will be consecrated by His glory" (Exodus 29:43). That word *consecrated* is the Hebrew transliteration *qadash*, meaning *to be set apart from*. It was after the sacrifices were made that God could then meet with his people and set them apart.

This was the covenant. It also required that the people could never meet one on one with God, and for that purpose, they had priests to serve as the *go between*.

God tells Moses in Exodus Chapter 25 what the Israelites are to bring as an offering. He tells Moses in verse 8 and 9:

"Then have them make a sanctuary for me, and I will dwell among them. Make this tabernacle and all its furnishings exactly like the pattern I have shown you".

This tabernacle was to be for God. May we never mistake that the tabernacles purpose was to bring glory to God. Therefore, presented to Moses were detailed blueprints of exactly how the Tabernacle was to be built. This wasn't to be merely a place, but a dwelling place for the Almighty. For that reason, it was to be constructed exactly as God intended. The Israelites were even instructed in what materials they would need to build with. God knew exactly what they were working with and exactly what was needed. They were given a divine plan that they were to follow exactly as prescribed.

Exodus goes into great detail, not only once, but twice on how the people are to build the tabernacle. Ten chapters separate the two sets of instructions that are almost exactly alike. The tabernacle would be a meeting place that could be transported. The walls are made of beautiful curtains made with blue, purple and scarlet yarn. The posts to hold the structure together were wooded posts. They filled the tabernacle with two separate areas, the outer court area and the holy area, which also contained the *Holy of Holies* that kept the Ark of the Covenant. In the Holy area was a table for bread, a lampstand and the altar of incense. The furnishings were made with gold and the finest materials. It always mystifies me how God is so great that He can lead a bunch of people, around two million former slaves, and He leads them into the desert, and they have exactly what they need to build a tabernacle. Not just sticks and stones, but with metals such as gold (Exodus 12:37).

My husband, a son of a preacher, for several generations on both sides, reminds me every time we sit through a church sermon that is focused on giving how difficult a message that is for a preacher. The first time he acknowledged that fact out loud, it completely caught me off guard. I guess I thought that was what every preacher wanted, and that they would brow beat you until you gave enough to help the church survive. My husband explained how his dad would agonize over looking at the bills of the church and the giving statements from that Sunday's service and realize how in the red the church was. He would watch his dad throughout the week as his dad distressed over how to get the funds to make ends meet without turning people away.

I love how God instructs Moses in chapter 25 to tell the Israelites to bring God an offering. He tells Moses that he will receive the offering from each man whose *heart prompts* him to give. God continues and tells Moses what to expect to receive from them. We aren't talking about checks, credit cards or cash. He tells Moses to expect gold, silver, blue, purple and scarlet yarn, goat hair, ram skins, acacia wood, onyx and other gems. These were very specific things that the Israelites were going to be giving Moses. Thank goodness we have a God who prompts hearts to get exactly what He needs to fulfill His purpose. I am sure that Moses was grateful as was Shane's dad, every time he witnessed God's provisions.

The author of Hebrews reiterates this point in Hebrews 8:5 when he calls the tabernacle a "copy and shadow of heaven." There was a reason it was so important to build the tabernacle exactly as God had instructed. There was a plan that was already laid out. God knew exactly what was going to happen. I wonder if Moses was ever tempted to add a little extra here or there only to find out that the materials weren't available.

As I watch my four-year-old son tear apart a package of Legos, I realize how awe struck the Israelites must have been. In the same way that a Legos package comes with exactly what is needed to build the picture on the front of the box so did the Israelite's have exactly what they needed to build this tabernacle. My son runs into problems building his Legos when he thinks he has a better plan than the Legos. We always remind him that if he's going to construct the object on the box, then he must do exactly as the instructions describe. It's hard for us to admit that the manufacturer knows better than us sometimes. In the same way, Moses is constantly reminded that they must build the tabernacle exactly as God has told them to do.

So often I find myself reading through this story, skipping over the significance of what is being described. There was a structure, not just four walls, but four walls that contained the Holiness of God. These people must have looked at this building like no other they had ever seen. They built this structure with their own hands, and it contained the Glory of God! I can just imagine their faces as they passed by, looking at this place that represented their freedom. It must have often been so meaningful to them at times they couldn't even comprehend how incredible God is. I often wonder if there were times when it just absolutely took their breath away. Were there people that when they walked by the temple, they would fall on their knees because they grasped the magnitude of what they were witnessing? Were people so caught up by the impact that they would walk by with tears of thankfulness? When they realized the greater plan, and the whole reason they had brought certain materials was to build a great dwelling place for God in the middle of a desert they must have been filled with awe. I often wonder if they stood outside and looked upon this tabernacle saying, "there is no one like you God" and believed it down to their core. <u>Could they have possibly taken God's presence for granted like we do every day?</u>

If you are familiar with the story, you already know that they continually tried to lean on their own understanding. The Israelites doubted that God would provide food; He delivered quall and manna right to them. Then, they decided that they needed to be able to see evidence of a god. So, they built a golden calf to worship. Not only were they worshiping idols, but they complained the whole way and doubted God's faithfulness and provisions. The wanted to believe that being an Egyptian slave was by far better than wandering in the desert. The saying *the grass is **always** greener on the other side* comes to mind.

Going back to Paul's statement of us, if I am truly a temple of the Holy God, I must be honest with myself and ask if I do the same despicable things as these Israelites. I may not live in a desert, and I may not be asking for quall and manna, and to deliver me to my promised land, but I do limit God in my life. I tell God what I can and cannot do. I tell Him what I do and do not want to do. I tell Him what is fair and what is not fair. I tell Him my plans, and I limit His potential in my life. I already have the excuses in my mind why I will or will not do certain things. In times of wandering, I question if I was better off where I was before, and I start to question the character of God. Yes, I do these same despicable things.

Interesting how our walk typically starts off with something that looks like the wandering tabernacle. God calls us to be His *treasured possessions* and if our hearts are soft, we answer with a *we will*, not having any idea what an awesome gift we have been given. We stumble in our sin and at times might wander off the course that was set for us.

One thing that stays constant is God is always dwelling within us, whether we acknowledge it or not.

In my early 20's, after going into the Air Force and struggling with some unfortunate events that happened in High School, I decided that a Holy God couldn't possibly love a sinner such as me. I figured He had left my *temple* a long time ago. I look back at this time period and remember going to church occasionally to be able to claim to be a *religious* person, whatever that means. I can't tell you much about the church service, the pastor, or any external detail of those occasions. What I can remember is sitting in the pews, choking my tears and emotions down. I had no idea why I would get so emotional in those moments until God revealed several years later that it was Him, calling my name. He wanted my heart. He wasn't going to smack me across the head, yell in my ear or beat a drum in my skull to get my attention. He is a God that whispers that He wants us. He loves us. He wants us to be a treasured possession. It is indeed the softest, gentlest, most loving request I have ever experienced. It is a call so sweet that it brings you to tears.

I would walk out of that church shoving so many emotions down, and I often wonder how sad that made God as He saw my heart yearning for what only He could give. Yet my pride lied to me to convince me that God didn't want me. Years later, after crying out to Him and asking where He had been for those years, He reminded me of those occasions in that little church in Cheyenne, Wyoming. He reminded me of the yearning in my heart. I had no idea at the time that it was Him.

God gave us a gift that the Israelites didn't have. When Jesus died on the cross and rose from the grave, we were given the gift of the Holy Spirit. It is a gift, given to anyone who believes. Just like the Israelites, I have been given all I need to get through this life. Just like the quail and manna that were free for the taking and they were given all that they needed and not a pinch more, so do I have. When I start telling God that I need more I become nothing more than the Israelites. Did the Israelites understand what they had and how precious it was? Do we know how special our bodies become as they fill with the precious Holy Spirit? Listening when the Spirit is trying to comfort a broken heart is a gift. Allowing the truth to be spoken into our minds from a Power greater than anything of this world is a gift. Relying on God's knowledge is our gift.

There has, and always will be a plan for your life and mine. It is already laid out. God has the tools to do whatever needs to be done to accomplish the goal. The magnificence for the Israelite's was never the desert. The beauty was what dwelled inside the tabernacle. That was the promise, and that was the gift. The gift today for us is the Holy Spirit. On the day of Pentecost, when the Spirit filled all the believers on the earth, Peter explained:

> *"Repent and be baptized, every one of you, in the name of Jesus Christ for the forgiveness of your sins. And you will receive the gift of the Holy Spirit. The promise is for you and your children and for all who are far off- for all*

whom the Lord our God will call" (Acts 2:38-39)

The gift was for all of us. This is one reason when talking to people about their struggles, I find myself often redirecting their questions. As they ask me questions, I turn them around and fire them back. Recently, I met with a lady struggling with just the mundane routines of life. She was asking me what kind of job she should take, if she should quit her current one, which daycare was best for her son, etc. I finally responded by asking her "These are all really good questions, but how is it that you make decisions?" She had the most confused look on her face, as I began to explain that these are questions that already have answers, answers of which I didn't know. She said she usually would just think about them and talk with her husband and then make the best decision possible. Sadly, this is how many of us who have been given the gift of the Holy Spirit make decisions. We hand our gift over as we decide what will be best for us when the Spirit is readily available to guide us through this process. It leaves us wandering like the stubborn Israelites.

Maybe, we need a new spin on this. Paul tells us later in 1 Corinthians, as he is talking about abstaining from sexual immorality that not only are our bodies a temple of the Holy Spirit and that we aren't even our own. He explains that we were bought at a price, and that is the reason why we are to honor Him with our bodies. We can turn down a gift, but if we aren't our own, then it's time to acknowledge the agreement that we have made. Something changes in my mind when I speak the words, "I am not my own, I have already been bought with a high price."

This mentality transforms my wandering tabernacle, to a permanently established temple. It creates in me confidence that I am not in this desert alone, but am filled with the Glory of God. Recently, I found myself in a position in which the authority over me was ultimately demanding that I either follow them or follow God. I found myself often in a controversy over whether to follow where I thought God wanted me, or follow the person of authority. For some reason, it never seemed to line up and mesh as it so often does when God is the center of both parties. Coming back to a whole relationship with God meant breaking the relationship off with that person. I had to pick God. What I realized was that I was letting other people tell me where God wanted me, and I realized that a relationship with God doesn't work that way. I had to tell myself over and over that the way it works is that God leads His people and we let the world know what we are doing, it doesn't work the other way around. I wonder how many of Christ's followers are in relationships such as this? How many of us are so deep in a manipulative relationship that we are completely lost in the desert? The spirit is a gift, it is our refuge, it is our strength in times of weakness, and it will lead us into our promised land. In the same way, I want to yell at the Israelites to obey the glory within the tabernacle, I often yell at myself to let my temple be led by the Spirit within.

We must ask ourselves why we fight obedience to an all-knowing God, who works all things for the good of those who follow Him? Could it be that we aren't aware of our bad decisions? It is so easy to point out the flaws of the Israelites, but in the Word of God, we are told that their hearts were hardened. They experienced the Glory of God, Moses saw God, and yet they still questioned Him. So, what should that tell us about our walk? In the book of Ephesians, we are told that a hardened heart results in living separate from God and living in a world of ignorance (Ephesians 4:18). I like Strong's Concordance translation of the word *ignorance* in that verse. It translates it into *willful blindness*. In Hebrews, we see that hardened hearts come from sin's deceitfulness (Hebrews 3:13), and Proverbs 28:14 states the consequence in black and white terms "but he who hardens his heart falls into trouble." Is it any surprise the Israelites were left for 40 years to wander in the desert? In the same sense, I must ask myself is it any wonder why I struggle for long durations of time? Is it possible that we not only fall victim to sin's deceitfulness but often choose willful blindness? I believe it is. We have a gift inside us that is better than anything else in this world, and yet the harsh reality of this world pushes us into making a choice based on fear. The first part of Proverbs 28:14, tells us the other option for overcoming a hardened heart; *"Blessed is the man who always fears the Lord."* Brown-Drivers-Briggs translates this word *fear* into a form that we will *deeply dread sin.* We will deeply dread the consequences the Lord will take to discipline us from our sin, and He will do that for the same reasons that we punish our own children. Love.

The tabernacle was a holy place that God made His presence known as it wandered through the desert. Doesn't that sound comparable to how Paul describes you and me?

CHAPTER THREE

EVERYTHING CAN BE TORN DOWN

Solomon's Temple

I wonder how many of us can relate to feeling like a temple that is wandering through a desert? Four-hundred and eighty years after the Israelites left Egypt; King Solomon built a majestic temple (1Kings 6:1). Reflecting greatly upon the blueprints of Moses Tabernacle, King Solomon's temple was almost twice as big.

Often with Christ followers, we don't love ourselves enough to allow our temples to become beautiful temples that are planted (having roots). This transition doesn't automatically happen either. This truly was a painful transition in my life.

For much of my early 20's, I was consumed with drinking, partying and having as much *fun* as I could. I was focused on all the things that continuously left me needing more. Instead of growing, these activities left me feeling emptier. By the grace of God, I got married to an amazing man. During this time, I was a drill sergeant in the Air Force and had no plans of settling down. I was a believer, but was struggling and was lost in the desert. I kept God at a distance because I was convinced that there was no way a Holy God could love a sinner as sinful as me. I was totally consumed with *my* plans for *my* life and kept striving to perform bigger and better to prove to Him that I wasn't as bad as I had convinced myself that I was. I told myself and God that I wasn't good enough to have kids or to be married. To sum it up, I chose to wander, just like the Israelites.

Over 400 years after the Israelites reached their promised land, we are introduced to King David and Solomon in the books of Samuel and Kings. The king at that time was King David. He declared that Solomon would be his successor at an early age. He recognized that Solomon was a man of great wisdom (1Kings 2:9). In fact, Solomon is known to have had the greatest wisdom in a man that has ever been or ever will be (1Kings 3:12). It had been a long time since the Israelite people had wondered in the desert and they began using the tabernacle for purposes that God hadn't designed it. There was no place that the people could centralize their worship, so for that purpose, Solomon set out to build a temple. Solomon's intention was that this to be a place where the people could worship and sacrifice in one location. He wanted to prevent the people from worshipping other gods. What eventually happened over the years was people were worshipping God still but started adding pagan worship as well. The need for this was recognized by David as well but wasn't something he was able to accomplish during his reign (1 Kings 8:19).

As the temple structure and furnishings are described throughout the Bible, it is easy for us to get lost in translation as the author uses words like cubits, portico, Parvaim, Cherubim and talk about shovels. However, one thing you won't miss as you read through the description of this temple was the ostentatious qualities throughout. This temple was three stories tall. You see the ceiling beams, doorframes, walls, and doors were overlaid with Gold (2 Chron. 3:7). This wasn't just a regular gold, but the gold of Parvaim, which is more precious than any other. He adorned the temple with precious stones and had a pair of Cherubim covered in this precious gold. These aren't little figurines that we are speaking of, but statues that have a wing span of 7.5 feet, all covered with gold. The curtains were made of fine linen with cherubim stitched into it. Most impressive in my mind was the *sea*, what we compare to a bathtub today, used for the ceremonial cleansing of the priests. This sea was a metal, circular basin. The rim was intricately designed with figures of bulls around it, and below the sea were twelve bulls, all facing out and the sea on top. The Bible states that the rim was comparable to a *"lily blossom"* and held about 17,500 gallons. In terms that we can understand today, that would be like a 27-foot, oval shaped pool that is one meter deep. Also furnished in the temple were basins used for washing the offerings, golden lampstands, gold sprinkling bowls and any other furnishings found in the temple of God (the tabernacle). Lastly, the ark of the Lord's covenant was brought to the temple. This is such a beautiful visual if you can imagine it; as the ark approached the temple, the Bible tells us that Solomon and the entire assembly of Israel were there offering sacrifice after sacrifice. So many sacrifices were made that day that the Bible tells us that they couldn't be counted or recorded. The people were doing this as a way of offering more than what was asked because they were so grateful to have a place of worship. As their hearts were filling with devotion to God, they couldn't stop offering more to God. I would wonder at some point if Solomon realized that whatever they offered to God in gratitude would never be sufficient?

Solomon likely went above and beyond what was expected because, in those days, a temple was what reflected the power of the god that it was dedicated to. King Solomon, with all his wisdom, likely realized that it was important to build this temple bigger, better and more impressive than any other for this reason. When the temple was finished, after seven years the cloud filled the temple and Solomon recognized the extraordinary work he had accomplished:

> *"I have indeed built a magnificent temple for you, a place for you to dwell forever" (1 Kings 8:12, 2 Chronicles 6:1)*

This temple was to be built to reflect the old tabernacle but to be far exceeding what anyone could expect, and it was intended to last forever. Solomon's goal was to build something that could be significant enough to reflect how awesome God is, but acknowledged that there is nothing on this earth that could do God justice. This would be simply an offering to God, as a place to worship and burn sacrifices to Him as a way of atonement for their sins (2 Chronicles 2:5-6). The purpose was to be the same as the tabernacle that the Israelites drug through the desert, but Solomon made it appear more majestic by the material things to please God.

Perhaps, the most descriptive part we read that shows the real emotions at the time is after the tabernacle is built. At this point, it is just a shell. It is a mere beautiful shell of a building. The people gather together, as we do for a grand opening of a hospital or a dedication of a church, and the Bible describes a beautiful coming together in honor of God:

> *"The trumpeters and singers joined in unison, as with one voice, to give praise and thanks to the Lord. Accompanied by trumpets, cymbals and other instruments, they raised their voices in praise to the Lord and say: He is good; his love endures forever" (2Chronicles 5:13)*

This cloud wasn't just an ordinary cloud, but it was a cloud filled with the Glory of the Lord. Can you imagine the magnitude of this sight? King Solomon, the greatest and wisest leader, stood and blessed the people, the whole assembly of Israel. He then got on the platform, and before all his people he knelt and spread his hands out to heaven as a way of giving all the credit to the One that deserved the worship. He showed the people that all the glory deserved to go to our God in heaven. This great king, on his knees, in front of all his people then says:

> *"O Lord, God of Israel, there is no God like you in heaven or on earth- you who keep your covenant of love with your servants who continue wholeheartedly in your way" (2 Chronicles 6:14)*

After praying, perhaps one of the most beautiful prayers ever prayed, the fire of the Lord came down and consumed the burnt offering and the sacrifices that were prepared for the Lord. The Glory of the Lord then filled the temple. When the crowd of people saw this, it drove them to their knees, and they worshipped and gave thanks to God. I can imagine these people on their knees so moved, so transformed by what they just witnessed that all they could get out was the words that we see in 2 Chronicles 7:3, "He is good; His love endures forever."

We should probably stop reading for a second to fully imagine the grandeur of this sight. This is so much more than just a casual conversation. A great king, offered the temple to the Lord, the cloud filled the temple, Solomon blessed the people and dedicated it through prayer to the Lord, the fire of the Lord consumed the offerings, and then the people fall on their faces. How I would have loved to be there witnessing this remarkable day. At the end of this great 14-day celebration we are told that the people left to go home "joyful and glad in heart for the good things the Lord had done" (2 Chronicles 7:10). Talk about a revival!

I wish from the bottom of my heart that I could experience such a sight. I think after 14 days of such an amazing sight, shared with so many people I would be one emotionally exhausted person.

As if all this wasn't enough, Chapter 7 continues with an answer from the Lord to Solomon, where he gives assurance to King Solomon that this temple won't be overlooked by God:

"I have chosen and consecrated this temple so that my Name may be there forever. My eyes and my heart will always be there" (2 Chronicles 7:16)

Such a beautiful story of promise to each other, it was a beautiful moment that has been shared with every generation since. I wish I could say that this all goes to a happily-ever-after ending. In the same way, I wish I could show someone my wedding videos and pictures and end the story with a … *happily-ever-after*. In fact, it was shortly after we were married that our lives turned upside down.

Shortly after our honeymoon to Jamaica, we were shocked to learn that we would be welcoming our first child before the first year had even passed. This happened contrary to what *my plan* for *my life* was. On our honeymoon to Jamaica, we brought back our first child, our daughter Charleigh Nicole. She was born on March 30th, 2007. I decided to separate from the Air Force. Looking back on that decision, I can't claim any part of it. It was a decision that I just felt *convinced* of. I have since recognized that it was God's leading being loud enough that my deaf ears could hear Him. This period of my life felt largely like the wandering in the desert. I look back now and see God's hand all over it, but I kept questioning Him and pushing Him farther away. I was as stubborn as the Israelites.

Five weeks after our precious daughter made her entrance into this world, May 9th, was a day when my fragile temple came crashing down. I made my way to take my college finals that morning at 10 a.m. I dropped my daughter off with a friend. I can still remember handing her over, and convincing myself that it was the right decision. Taking college finals compared to taking care of my newborn seemed so insignificant. How in the world was I to care about a test when I could witness the hand of God before me? Could the face of my little angel compare to what the Israelites witnessed in the tabernacle? Could the emotion of looking upon the face of something that I never planned on or could take credit for, but definitely came from me compare to the tabernacle? Nevertheless, I left her and drove to take my finals. I remember pulling out of the driveway telling myself to focus on my finals, and I'll be back in no time to pick that little piece of Heaven up. I was thoroughly convinced after she was born that she was a gift from above.

On her birth announcement, we put *"All God's grace in one little face."* I have no idea how I knew she was such a gift before that fateful day, but perhaps it was because after she was born, I was so grateful for her and knew she was never in *my plan.* It was five weeks later that I understood just how much of a gift she was.

We were living in San Antonio at the time, and as I drove through the city on the four lanes of Highway 90, I began to merge right to make my exit. A man was standing on the side of the road, and in a city the size of San Antonio, this is not a rare occurrence. He was just innocently standing there. I often wander what he was thinking in those moments. Were his thoughts focused on getting across the busy eight lane interstate to reach the bus depot on the other side? Was he focused on getting to someone's house, maybe a loved one's house? Maybe he was focused on getting to the hospital to visit a sick friend? Was he contemplating the difference between taking his chances and running across the intersection or going down and crossing at the underpass because he was late meeting someone? Maybe he was late for a job interview? Or, maybe he was late for a volunteer opportunity to serve the homeless downtown? His thoughts are captive to him and God alone. How often I wonder what thoughts were going through his mind. Was he convincing himself that his life had no meaning, no purpose and that maybe life would be better without him in it? I will never, never know until one sweet day when my mind is flooded with all answers to these questions.

Whatever his thoughts were, they made him take his last several steps onto the busy interstate. They must have been so impactful that they convinced his body to take the chance on this busy interstate. I think it was a split second of disbelief as I watched his body step out onto the interstate in front of me. It's the split second that anyone can speculate on what they would do, but will never know until they are behind the wheel at that exact moment, at that exact place. The mind is a powerful tool. My mind quickly calculated the fact that the place where the man was, and the point where I was would collide regardless of the amount of pressure put on the brakes, and the better option was to swerve as far left as I could without hitting anyone else. For a fraction of that second, I must have felt relief that I would miss this man and could go about with my college finals. This is truly because your mind can never fathom the other possibility.

I wish I could say that is what happened. If my life happened as I calculated and dictated I wouldn't be here with a story to tell. If my calculating mind always predicted the path accurately my temple wouldn't have been crushed that day. What I didn't calculate was the fact that this man would decide to run across. Again, I wonder what his last thoughts were. Could they have been to hurry up because a car was coming to avoid impact or was it indeed to ensure impact? What I do know is that he never once looked at me. He never looked into my eyes. He never made a living connection with the person that I am. Does he just know me by the blue Dodge Charger that I was driving that day? Or did he even look in my direction, cautious of me at all?

The impact was sudden. His face hit right in front of mine, not even two feet away, leaving the shape of a bowl in the shattered windshield. His body flew up and to the left. His white shoe flew over the car and landed behind it. I can't tell you what I thought in those moments. I'm sure my mind wasn't accepting what had happened.

After so many years of first responder training in the Air Force, I remember knowing how important it was going to be to get help. I immediately grabbed my cell phone as I frantically waived for the passing traffic to stop. I ran over to the man who laid so still on the ground. When I got to him, I looked in his eyes that stared so blankly into the blue sky. I asked him "Are you okay?" It seems like the most bizarre question to ask him as I know that I knew, in fact, he wasn't okay. It felt like an eternity of trying to make a connection with 9-1-1 and getting someone to stop. I remember feeling a horrific panic as I thought I would never get any help.

Within moments a priest pulled up, quickly followed by an off-duty Air Force EMT. They immediately began CPR. The priest prayed a blessing over the body, and everything else is a blur during this time to me. People ran over from surrounding businesses. One man was from an auto body shop. He had witnessed the accident. I remember him grabbing me and hugging me as if I was someone who mattered to him. I was a complete stranger to him. The priest put me in his car, and I sat there crying, not knowing how to even open my eyes. His wife sat in the front seat not knowing what to say. She sat there with the compassionate love and concern in her eyes, not having any words that would begin to help. She told me over and over it was going to be alright. I handed my phone to someone, and he called my husband for me. I have no clue how he even knew what name to search. I couldn't breathe as I sat there. As I write these words, through tear filled eyes, I wish I could express on this paper the amount of love I have for these random people. These strangers that loved me enough to stop and help me that day. These faces that I love that have no names to go with them. I bet they remember me too.

Shortly after they started CPR, I asked one of the people on the site how the man was, still obviously in complete denial. This stranger who has no name or face to go along with the impact that he had in my life had to tell me that the man had died and that they stopped CPR. The response that came from my own mouth was what sounded like a cry of anguish, it was a plea to God to make this all okay, begging God to let this man get up and walk away. Unfortunately, that wasn't what happened. It wasn't part of the plan. That sunny, warm and beautiful spring morning in May held a different, more tragic plan for my life.

As the police and ambulance came and the other people began to leave, a news crew also showed up. I was put in the ambulance until my husband arrived to avoid the media. I remember walking to the ambulance and realizing that a white body bag replaced the spot I expected to see the man lying. I also noticed the white shoe still lying in the same place on the road.

That day, I learned what it felt like to feel like your soul is crushed. All that I had seemed lost. Everything that I had put in to make this person all that I had become fell apart in a matter of a second. My success, my education, my house, my possessions all instantly became nothing. They didn't save me, nor did they offer any promise of hope.

King Solomon in the Old Testament would likely be able to relate to that feeling as he watched the beautiful temple he had meticulously built torn down in an instant.

King Solomon's reign was 40 years long. He poured his heart into following God, and after having a beautiful relationship, we read that his heart turned away from the Lord (1 Kings 11:9). After witnessing Solomon and God's conversation and the love that was exchanged, we read that the Lord appeared not only once, but twice to Solomon. It should sadden all of us as we read that Solomon's heart turned against God. Solomon couldn't resist the temptations to worship other gods, and it rightfully angered the one true God. It is one of the characteristics that I didn't understand about God until recently. I initially would have read that God was angered and became withdrawn a little from the fact that God is easily angered. I read that today and am filled with so much gratitude and love. The reason is this; what would it say about God if it didn't bother Him that His dearly loved Solomon was worshipping other gods. It would be like a wife or a husband who wasn't angered by a cheating spouse. We would likely assume that God is lackadaisical with His love. We know though that it is God's abounding love that separates Him from any other. He loves so intently that when one of His beloveds stray, He follows them. He fights for them. He gets angry. For that, we say thank you God for getting angry when I stray so that I'm not lost forever in my sin.

There are so many of us that believe Satan's lie that we are alone in our struggle with sin and turning our hearts away from God. God appeared to Solomon, and he still turned away from God. Accept your struggle and realize it is a struggle for all of us, the powerful, the weak, the rich, and the poor. You can live in a grand mansion with all the possessions you ever dreamed of and still fall victim to sin. The good news for all of us is that God is pursuing us right now in the midst of our sin. We can know for certain, that we are never, ever alone.

Because of Solomon's sin, God split the kingdom in two. Through the next 350 years, God's chosen people suffered because of their sin. Jerusalem ends up falling in 586 B.C. to the Babylonian King Nebuchadnezzar. At this time the King of Jerusalem was King Zedekiah. We are told that King Zedekiah was no better than the sinful kings that reigned before him. He was a young king, and during his reign, the amount of sin resulted in God "thrusting them from his presence" (2 Kings 24:19).

The Babylonians were cruel, and they destroyed the city. Scripture tells us that they killed King Zedekiah's sons before him and put out his eyes as they took him captive to suffer the last horrific sight he was to see for the rest of his life. We are told that the Babylonian army burned the city. They burned the temple down. This was the same temple that held the Glory of our Lord, and where we saw Solomon and the Lord brought together. The Babylonian army tore the temple apart seeking the monetary riches the items would bring rather than the supreme importance of the items. We read of this devastation in 2 Kings 25:13-16:

> *"The Babylonians broke up the bronze pillars, the movable stand and the bronze Sea that were at the temple of the Lord and they carried the bronze to Babylon. They also took away the pots, shovels, wick trimmers, dishes and all the bronze articles used in the temple service. These commanders of the imperial guard took away the censers and sprinkling bowls- all that were made of pure gold and silver. The bronze from the two pillars, the sea and the movable stands, which Solomon had made for the temple of the Lord, was more than could be weighed."*

We also read that they took the priests captive as well. There was nothing left. The temple was ravaged. The Babylonian army didn't stop to consider the inherent value this building had to these people. They didn't get it, nor did they care. The Babylonians' intention was to devastate, embarrass and destroy these people.

We read this and wonder, *who would do such a thing to God's beautiful temple?* This world is cruel. We live in this same cruel world. God's temple gets torn down every second of every day, my friend. The walls of his children (temples) come tumbling down, and so often we stand in horror. We wonder why He would allow this to happen to us? In an instant, one phone call, one diagnosis, one knock on the door and our temples come crashing down.

I remember on the morning of May 9th, I sat in the back of the ambulance wondering this same question. Wondering how in the world I could be doing everything right and in an instant, have my temple torn down. I realize that God is in control every second of every day, so why did He allow my world to come crashing down? And why didn't anything that I had built my life around save me from this? Why didn't being a *good person* or being *successful* protect us from tragedy? Did the people of Jerusalem cry the same prayer I did on my fateful morning? Is this the same prayer maybe you have prayed one momentous day as well?

As I sat in the back of the ambulance staring at my feet, trying to remember how to just open my eyes and breath, my husband, my gift from God, appeared in the door. He climbed in the back of the ambulance in his military uniform with the most concerned look on his face. I said the words for the first time in genuine confusion, "Shane, I've killed someone." There was no explanation to give or any defense. There was no way to explain what happened. He didn't have any questions at that moment. I assume there was nothing which seemed relevant to ask. It was a minute that we sat in complete silence as we held on to each other in hopes that maybe our love would erase what just happened.

I remember this moment better than any other moment. I remember the look on my husband's face that said Shane was as devastated and lost as I was. I wonder as the people in Jerusalem heard the news that day if they also had devastation written across their face? In that split second, if they realized all they had that they took for granted was now all gone.

In Kay Arthur's bestselling, historical novel she recounts this piece of the story by putting into a fictionalized sense:

> *"The Chaldeans had come over the city wall and were marching through Jerusalem in seemingly endless ranks. They descended like locusts, devouring every home with fire and striking every man, woman, and child in their path with their swords. No enemy eye took pity; no one was spared. Innocent babies- their little bodies impaled on Chaldean swords- were mercilessly paraded through the streets with shouts of victory only to be tossed aside when a new victim was discovered".*
> *(Israel, My Beloved, pg 49)*

This had to have been devastating for the people to witness such cruelty. Kay goes on to take captive their thoughts during the devastation:

"There's nothing to live for; there never will be. I've been ruined for life. What was left of my hope has perished in these streets." (Israel, My Beloved, pg 51)

As I read those words on the page, it struck me that those are the words I told myself sitting in the back of that ambulance. My world felt like it was over, but my body somehow remained on this earth. I instantly turned from an ambitious, goal oriented person into an individual who was just finding a way to take one step at a time. In my mind, I thought they may as well take me to jail because my life seemed like it was destined for misery. The turmoil of living inside bars appeared to be a relief when compared to the anguish my heart felt. What I heard next shocked me. The police officer told me I could go home and asked what I would like him to do with my car? I wanted to beg him to take me to jail. It would have been easier to have been guilty of doing something wrong than to have no explanation or reasoning behind it. My expression must have said it all because he continued, "You have to go home. You did nothing wrong". As far as the car went, I never wanted to see it ever again. I wanted to tell him to throw it in a dump so dark and bottomless as to never to be seen again.

That car meant something to me at one time. A week before Shane and I got married we traded his truck in for this pretty blue Dodge Charger. We were so excited to be together and starting our life together, after being separated by military obligations for a year that we decided we deserved a new vehicle to kick off our new life. In fact, we were so blinded by love that we were taken to the bank on this car. To be completely honest, we never cared. The following week, we drove that car all the way from Texas to Utah where on the top of a mountain in Southern Utah, we exchanged our vows and promised before our closest family and friends that we would love each other until death do us part. On the way to the mountain where our wedding took place, my dad drove me in my beautiful wedding dress in that car. I remember how we discussed the weather and commented on the beauty of the mountains to avoid any emotions sitting in that car. After Shane and I had exchanged vows, we got in that same car, with writing all over the windows and drove to the most meaningful dinner and dance I've ever been to. A year later, we drove our precious Charleigh Nicole home from the hospital in that car. We were two brand new parents, nervous about every bump and sound as we drove the baby home. I remember sitting in the back to make sure she was alright and looking at Shane through the rearview mirror with pure astonishment of our new family member. So, to say this car didn't matter wouldn't reflect appropriately upon our life. It was a possession that was associated with the memories of being blessed by God. On May 9th, that car became something I never wanted to see again. The memories that were stirred up within me when I looked at it seemed to cancel out any good that came from it. When the devastation feels like all hope has been taken away and it would hurt worse to continue to live than to give it up, cars and happiness become distant memories.

We know a military couple that one day their life was great and the next morning their six-month-old never woke up. I know that you know someone like that too. I can only imagine that the importance of things to people like that matters little right now. The military couple we know would give it all up to have their boy back. In fact, I have never been more confident of an answer, and I would never have asked them that question. The same can be assumed of the Israelites as they lost everything. It wasn't the gold and jewels they mourned, but the loss of a temple that contained the Lord. It was the people that were lost. This is a universal truth that will be forever true for all of humanity, regardless of what generation we are part of. For me, it's the evidence that we are all more than just creatures that have evolved through time. It is the evidence of a God who created us with purpose and in His image.

The book of Ezekiel is a fascinating book, written by the Prophet Ezekiel before, during and after the fall of Jerusalem. He warned them that they would be judged, then he warned how they were judged, and then finally he warned them that God was with them even after they were judged, living in captivity in Babylon. Ezekiel tells of a man dressed in linen with a writing kit which was sent by God. He was directed to go throughout the city and put a mark on the foreheads of those who were righteous. These people God made clear wouldn't be touched, but the rest would be killed. Ezekiel chapter nine is a hard chapter to read, as we see the righteous protected and the rest slaughtered. At one point Ezekiel tells us that he falls to his face crying out for mercy from the Lord. The chapter ends with the man in linen saying "I have done as you have commanded." What a sad chapter of the Bible. We witness the consequences of the sin the Israelites have continually chosen over God, the God that promised to love them forever and pulled them from slavery into a promised land.

Ezekiel describes the glory of the Lord departing from the Temple in Chapter 10. He describes watching the Cherubim as they carried the glory of the Lord away. They didn't look back, hesitate or circle the temple, but went straight ahead. Without any apprehension, the glory of the Lord got up and left that place that stood so beautifully at one time and was now filled with dead bodies.

The people of Jerusalem that survived the invasion became servants to the Babylonian king. They became captives for the next 70 years (2 Chronicles 36:20).

When my temple came tumbling down on May 9th, my heart became captive to the destruction that ruled my life. I didn't make a choice that morning to make a change. I didn't see two paths and choose the one that led to pain. That decision was made for me, and my heart felt as if it was held captive. The time period for the people of Jerusalem was 70 years. The same could have been true in my life. I could still be held in captivity. Seventy years from the day it happened would put me at 95 years old. That is entirely possible. It is my choice.

Periods of captivity are not ideal. Being held captive, you focus on wanting to breathe. Your attention stays directed to survival. These aren't times of productivity, but of existence. Behind every smile is a tear. The future is non-existent; goals are unimportant, and hope is lost. Captivity becomes consumed by a life of survival.

We are told in scripture that during this period the vacant land left in destruction enjoyed its Sabbath rest (2 Chronicles 36:21). The people are instructed way back in the day of Moses to let their fields rest every seven years as a way to respect God (Leviticus 24:4). Over the years, the people had disregarded this command along with many others. God warned them that the land would be overtaken and would take its Sabbath years during that time. Should it be any surprise that we find hundreds of years later that this is what happened to the land? Those 70 years of captivity, the land stayed dormant.

I love the analogy that this plays in my life and that in the Bible these periods are called *Sabbath rests*. When I think of a Sabbath, I associate that word with God in the very beginning of the Bible when He creates the world and everything it contains and then on the seventh day He takes a break (Sabbath). Sabbath means a time of rest. Whether this season is a day, a month, or seventy years, it is a Sabbath. When our world comes falling down, it's important to take a season of rest. Our first thoughts can't be about how to escape the pain, but to rest, and I will tell you the most comforting place to rest is in the precious arms of God. A Sabbath is a good thing. We are told that these Sabbath rests are "Holy to the Lord" (Exodus 31:15). Not only is this time important to us for resting, but it is important to the Lord. It's in our faith that we rest in Him. It is often so easy to believe that during this time that we don't matter to God, and that He has forgotten about us. On the contrary, we see the Israelite land that a season of rest was the best thing that could have happened after it was overtaken by the Babylonians. It requires faith to rest and to wait for the healing.

Captivity doesn't have to last forever. For the Israelites, in 2 Chronicles we see a hint of hope, a glimmer of light at the end of the tunnel. We read that God moves the heart of the King of Persia, King Cyrus.

The evidence of God moving him is evident as we read the King's proclamation:

> *"The Lord, the God of heaven, has given me all the kingdoms of the earth and he has appointed me to build a temple for him at Jerusalem in Judah. Anyone of his people among you may the Lord his God be with him, and let him go up" (2 Chronicles 36:23)*

This hope to the people is the same hope that you and I hold. There will be a time to rebuild our lives. The Sabbath is called a *period* of rest because it was never meant to last forever. Someone (or something) comes along and brings hope back into our hearts. A piece of hope is where it all begins. It's not a leap into being totally better, but it may be the largest leap that we will ever take. I know the difficulty of Sabbath is this; you don't get to see the mighty hand of God working. That is why it is called a Sabbath. We start to wonder if God is still here with us, or if He has deserted us. The promise that He gave to Solomon after Solomon dedicated the temple to the Lord is the same promise we must hold on to. God makes a promise to Solomon that His eyes and heart will always be there.

As our empty temples are destroyed, and we are trying to remember how to survive, we have to bear in mind that God's eyes and heart will always be with us.

CHAPTER FOUR

COURAGE TO REBUILD WHAT WAS ONCE BEAUTIFUL

Rebuilding the Temple

Perhaps the hardest experience that we endure in this life is losing our loved ones. A friend of mine had a healthy, adorable baby boy. After several months of adoring her little fellow, she noticed he was having issues with his eyes. His tiny body slowly degenerated until he was deaf and blind. He was never diagnosed with anything that would explain his condition. He lived for 12 precious years, with his mom, dad and sister loving him through every day until he took his last breath. I met this woman about six months after she lost her boy. I saw the remains of a temple destroyed. Over the next several years I watched as his mother allowed her temple to be rebuilt. It started at the eight-month mark when she agreed to speak at a retreat about her boy and the journey she was on. As she sat there explaining that she was just learning how to breath and escape the captivity of a broken heart, I was reminded that rebuilding something that has been torn down is a painful process that takes time. Knowing what was and what was lost, yet finding the courage to accept the change is a hard process.

Just recently I went to a funeral for a high school girl who died in a car accident. At the funeral, I could see the temples tumbling. Losing such a sweet girl at such a young age just doesn't make sense to those of us left behind. Eighteen short years is just never enough, and those that poured love into her life are left wondering how to move on without her. Is there any hope as we all struggle through the confusion of why this would happen? Is it possible to believe that the temple can be rebuilt for so many that will change drastically from such a tragic loss? As I sat at the funeral watching the high school choir sing a beautiful song they wrote for this young lady, I wondered; *is it actually possible after such a devastating week for these young people to become better because of it?* Can they pick up the pieces and rebuild the heart that was so innocently and perfectly created?

We all know incredible people, who are strong believers who we think are unshakeable. Just when we begin to think that they are so holy that God will protect them, the walls come down. Watching Rick Warren's journey has been incredible for me. He influences so many lives that you would think that surely God will protect him. We have all seen him deal with his adult child committing suicide. We all know how awesome he was before the accident, and then we have watched him as he has dealt with the loss and rebuilt his beautiful temple. Perhaps he is more influential today than ever.

After 70 years of captivity, the people of Jerusalem stepped out of captivity. It marked the beginning of a whole new life for the captives. The possibility of rebuilding suddenly became possible. In an instant, the Israelites' purpose transformed from a life of mere survival to one of absolute freedom.

Stepping out of captivity is the largest step we can take. It's the difference between everything. It marks the difference between going forward or backward, sinking or rising, red and green, darkness or light. That first step out of captivity may be the greatest, and possibly the hardest.

After the Persian King, Cyrus defeated the Babylonians we are told that the Lord moved King Cyrus's heart to send the captives back to their home land and to aid them in the rebuilding efforts of the temple (Ezra 1:1). We are told that God moved the hearts of the people that He needed to return to accomplish His will. God even touched the hearts of others around them to provide the items required to rebuild that temple. He made their path clear, for them to accomplish His will.

It wouldn't do the story adequate justice if we didn't attempt to dive into the emotional aspect of what these people were going through. After 70 years (yes, that would be a lifetime for most of us) had passed, many of these people were unfamiliar with what and where their homeland even was. These people had been violently taken captive and had suffered at the hand of the Babylonians. King Cyrus was telling them to return to an unfamiliar place for some, and the rest had significant emotional baggage associated with this land. This land to the latter group represented defeat, captivity, and remembrance of their loved ones brutally killed. King Cyrus was telling a beaten down group of captives, mere slaves to return to their war-ravaged land and to rebuild. In the book of Ezra, we find the list of people who bravely returned to this land. We are told there were over 42,360 captives that returned to their land (Ezra 11:64).

In our attempt to empathize with this group of people, you ask yourself *"If you were one of these returning captives, what is the first thing you would be likely to do?"* You may be surprised to learn the first thing that the returning captives did. After settling in their towns, we are told that they began to rebuild the altar. The Bible doesn't tell us of a celebration happening at this point. No musical instruments are playing, nor dancing in the streets, but we are told that:

"Despite the fear of the peoples around them, they built the altar on its foundation and sacrificed burnt offerings on it to the Lord"
Ezra 3:3

As these brave people picked up their tools and supplies, they laid the foundation. Then they built the altar. We read that the people around them were scared. The Hebrew word that we see here for *fear* means that these onlookers weren't only afraid, but were terrified, they were filled with dread as they watched these brave individuals build this altar. The chosen people were making a statement that they were laying a permanent foundation, and were staying. They would worship their God again, despite the memories that haunted them. They would worship an almighty God, notwithstanding their hardship of the last 70 years. No matter what people around them thought, or the dread they stirred in hearts of those around them, they would build. They would build the one thing that would show their devotion and love to our God. This type of strength, a strength only God can give, will bring fear in those who don't understand.

We are told that after they had built their altar, the people celebrated with offerings. The first thing they observed was the Feast of Tabernacles, which was a seven-day celebration that was typically held at the end of the growing season to celebrate all that God had given them. Can you imagine what celebrating the end of a season of captivity meant? Can you imagine the celebration of all God had brought them through? On their minds were probably the faces of people that didn't live through the captivity, thinking "*If they could have only lived to see this!*" To only ponder the amount of emotion they were filled with as they watched the required sacrifices go up in flames on that altar that they built with their own hands. After those seven days of celebration, they presented the burnt offerings. They led the perfect bulls, rams or male birds to the altars where they let the fire entirely consume the animals as a sign of their voluntary acts of worshiping God. Can you imagine the animal's screams as they were consumed by fire? Blood had to be shed for their sins. Burnt offerings were symbolic, the people were giving their full dedication and devotion to God, and they were sorry for any unintentional sin they may have committed. By these offerings, they were saying ***"We are ready to fully surrender to You, God."*** They then presented sacrifices for all the sacred feasts of the Lord.

Can you imagine this sight? Can you imagine the on-lookers filled with more dread as the sacrifices go on?

Next, the foundation was laid. As it was poured the people began celebrating singing *"He is good, His love to Israel endures forever"* (Ezra 3:11). There was a great celebration following the victory. However, not everyone was celebrating. The Word tells us that there was a group of people that mourned. These people were the older priests and Levites and family heads who had seen the temple that Solomon had built. As these people watched the foundation being built for this temple, they remembered. They were thinking of the greatness of their old temple. They remembered the work that went into it. They remembered the pride of standing outside and admiring its beauty. They remembered the feeling of awe as they knew it contained the Glory of God. They remember hearing and watching as it was torn down. They remember seeing their captors parading the precious furnishings through the streets as if they were worth nothing more than a monetary value. Realizing that the supplies they had would compare nothing to what was needed to rebuild a temple as grand as the last one, caused more weeping. They mourned what was.

After being released from the accident sight, my husband asked me what we should do. We sat in the seat of his truck, and I had no idea. I did know that only two things mattered to me at that moment. Those two things were my husband and my daughter. The two things that I look back and realize that I can take no credit for either.

When my husband proposed to me, he was kneeling in a pile of horse poop and had caught me off guard. My response to his question was "*I don't know*" at which time I received a **God thump** and quickly answered "Y*es*". After being married, I was convinced that I didn't want children. I was way too preoccupied with being in the military to have time to rock babies to sleep. Perhaps, I never considered becoming a mother because deep down I realized I couldn't even love myself. After being married for a matter of days, we got pregnant on accident.

The two things I had no idea that I wanted became all that mattered to me at that moment.

We immediately drove back to our friends' house where I left my daughter and ran in and grabbed her. As I looked at her precious face, I knew that I would survive. I had to. I had to figure this out for her. It wasn't just about me anymore.

We got back to our house, and within an hour we had a pastor at our home. He sat there looking at me as I asked him for all the answers that I thought he was there to deliver. How am I supposed to move on? How do I go about my life now? Why did this happen to me? Why would God do this to me? Does God really love me, because it sure doesn't feel like it? Can I ever figure out who that man that I hit was? How can I reach out to the family and tell them how sorry I am?

How do I continue with life in a normal manner when I don't think anything matters anymore? As the questions continued, I found myself frustrated at His lack of being able to fill the emptiness inside me. It was almost a relief when he left because the longer he was there, the more it began to sink in that he didn't have a clue how to answer these questions.

My initial plan for that day was to take my finals then return home with the baby and clean the kitchen. As the house cleared, I just couldn't bring myself to do it. It seemed so pointless. Who cares about the cleanliness of a kitchen when there was a family that lost a son, brother, and friend?

I remember it beginning to sink in that I would never be the same. I knew who that person was before 10 a.m. that morning, but suddenly I became a stranger in my own skin. The unknown was scary as I wondered who I was to become. I began to mourn what was.

Mourning as they watched the new temple being built makes all too much sense. They are rebuilding because the last one was torn down. It became a victory and heartache all in one. Even if I knew what God was going to build in me from that experience, I didn't want to build a new temple either. I wanted the old me back.

The Bible tells us the sound that came from God's chosen was so loud that it was impossible to distinguish between the cries of victory and the cries of weeping. Try as you might imagine this scene, as confusing as it must have been. Some cheering over the delight of the victory, while others are mourning the loss of what was lost.

What a sight this must have been for those that didn't understand what was going on. In the same way, my recovery was very scary for those around me. There was a significant internal battle being waged over my soul that I couldn't explain to people at the time. The dark times were dark and the happy times were few.

A few days after the accident, we got a rental car as our car would be several weeks getting fixed. I was encouraged to drive again as soon as possible. It became one of those days that was scary for those around me.   Shane and I drove out on a deserted highway in South Texas, and as I got behind the wheel for the first time, I remember gripping the steering wheel hard with both hands. As I began driving, tears filled my eyes. I was mad. Angry at the fact that around the corner someone could jump out in front of me and there was nothing I could do to stop it. I was mad that I had no control over my life. I was angry that someone else could make a decision that could wreck my life forever and instantly tear the wall of my temple down.

On a trip north of San Antonio, I remember fighting sleep as my husband drove us along. I would shut my eyes, and they would pop right back open. I was scared to shut them as I didn't know if I would ever have a chance to see the light of day again. What if we were in a horrible accident and the last thing I saw was whatever I looked at before I fell asleep? If time was so precious who would want to spend it sleeping anyway? I realized just how out of control my life was. The battle was internal for me and scary for those who were around me. There was nothing they could do to help.

A most interesting thing happens when the Israelites' enemies find out that they are building a temple. They offer to help. Their explanation for wanting to help was:

> *"Let us help you build because like you, we seek your God and have been sacrificing to him since the time of Esarhaddon king of Assyria, who brought us here" Ezra 4:2*

I'm sure you are thinking the same thoughts that I think as I read this; that more hands make for lighter work, right? Wrong. The Israelites answer their enemies with a statement that we all need to burn into our soul, store in our memories and guard with an appreciation for what it means:

> *"You have no part with us in building our temple to our God. We alone will build it for*

the Lord, the God of Israel, as King Cyrus, the King of Persia commanded us." Ezra 4:3

You see, it's the same thing that I learned as I struggled. My temple was torn down, and as much as I would have loved for someone to come and help rebuild it, it was mine and mine alone. The work wasn't something I could have given someone else. Trust me when I say that I begged to hand it over to someone every morning as I opened my exhausted eyes and faced reality all over again. It was exhausting. The fact remains, though that our temple is our temple alone, and we are individually commanded to rebuild it. Don't get me wrong, it is crucial to find people who can help, but help is merely that...help.

For the Israelite people, there may have been several reasons why they denied the help. First, they had to question the motives of these people. Was their real intention to help a group of exiles who were building a temple for God? Were they so moved with happiness over watching this victory from a group of former slaves that they were invested in the construction of a bigger temple? Remember, these were most likely the same people that were filled with dread watching the altar being built. Most likely these people were willing to help strictly for political reasons. These onlookers probably watched these people struggle and figured if they could contribute to and gain the support of the group it would eventually help them in their level of influence over the land. Perhaps, their real motives were to sabotage the building of the temple.

Secondly, the Israelites may have denied help because they realized the importance for the Israelites to maintain the religious purity in their temple. By allowing the involvement of these other religious groups, they would risk falling into the same trap of idol worship that had led to their demise 70 years earlier. They realized that what happened in the temple was something they couldn't risk handing over to foreigners.

Finally, it is possible the Israelites denied help because they acknowledged that God had commanded them to build the temple. He didn't charge the bystanders with that responsibility. He instructed the exiles, and they were listening after 70 years of realizing what disobedience leads to. King Cyrus was very specific about who was to build the temple. The Israelite people weren't likely willing to risk this opportunity by disobeying.

Those three reasons are perfect reasons for us to focus on taking the reins in each of our journeys through this life. Particularly, when our temple gets torn down, people will come with the most outlandish advice. They will often direct you in the wrong direction. Often this looks like actions rooted in hatred, discord, jealousy, fits of rage, selfish ambitions, and dissension (see the acts of sinful nature Galatians 5:19-21). If they aren't speaking from a Holy Spirit perspective, it is necessary to proceed with caution as to how much influence they get in your life. I can remember walking away from many people thinking, "*They just don't get it.*" Many people had the perfect answer for me, "*It wasn't your fault.*" In response, I would think, "*Yeah, I know that, but it doesn't change the fact that I killed someone.*" Advice that leads you astray will suck any religious purity from you, and we point at Satan for this corruption. Caution must be exercised in replacing anything in your life with shoes that only God can fill. God has commanded us to live certain lives that are contrary to what our sinful natures want to follow, and these are decisions that we can't entrust to anyone, but ourselves. The easy answers and solutions to our problems aren't always the right path, for God calls us to walk in love. For example, the world tries to convince us to push any blame off onto everyone around us, but God commands us to forgive.

There's a story in the New Testament about a man named Simon. Simon was a sorcerer and would amaze the people that watched him with his sorcery. However, he was unable to impact the people the way that Peter and John could when they laid their hands upon the people, and the people received the Holy Spirit. Simon was jealous of this power and offered to pay them for it. Peter responded:

"You have no part or share in this ministry, because your heart is not right before God. . . For I see that you are full of bitterness and captive to sin" Acts 8:21-23

Recovery is a miraculous event. When it is accomplished it will be something no one can take credit for, but God. He leads you out of captivity and gives you the materials to rebuild. For my friend who lost her little boy, watching her recovery was nothing that anyone could have given her. She is a strong, amazing, beautiful woman today because through the experience she didn't sacrifice her purity to take an easy way out. The confidence she carries today you can tell is a divine gift. Those who witnessed her journey stand back and say, "*Now, that is a God thing.*"

God will provide people to walk through the journey with us as well. He provided me some amazing people to help me wade through the devastation from a broken heart. I knew two things about these people. First, they had a heart for God.

DEARLY LOVED EXILE

Secondly, they may not have been perfect, but the fruit of the spirit was evident especially in the way that they changed my life by their words. I would have been suffocated if I hadn't allowed these people in my life. Sometimes this means we need to reach out to people for help. I found myself tempted to completely shut down to everyone in my life and that wasn't what God wanted either. We all know those people though that are hurt, and so they shut everyone out.

When the Israelite people got ready to build the altar, it says in chapter 3, verse 1 that after they settled in the land *"the people assembled as one man in Jerusalem."* This is what it will feel like when God has brought people into your life to help guide you in finding your freedom. It will feel like they have jumped in the devastation and have grabbed your hand to help you find your way out. They will have a flashlight in a dark and damaged world. Some flashlights are brighter than others, but they all help illuminate a world that longs for light.

These people are truly the light of the world. I have met many religious people who can tell you anything you want to know about grace, sin, etc., but when it comes to action, they leave you less than enthralled. The light of the world type people are the people we read about in the gospels when Jesus is on the cross:

> *"Near the cross of Jesus stood his mother, his mother's sister, Mary the wife of Clopas, and Mary Magdalene." John 19:25*

We may fall into the same lies that many people fall into when they see someone in the midst of tragedy. The lies go like this, *"They won't notice me,"* or *"There's nothing I can do to help,"* or *"I don't know what to say."* We are told in scripture that Jesus *saw* his mother there and the disciple whom He loved standing nearby. Can you imagine the comfort that He had just knowing people loved Him enough to stand amidst a crowd that hated Him? People were willing to step out for Him. That's usually all we need, is to see someone standing there. It takes courage, though, the same courage that a lot of the *religious* are lacking.

This lack of courage is what keeps us from being the light of the world. I recently had an opportunity to be part of a church that lost a key member. I was saddened by the way it was dealt with. As so many hearts broke and the devastation was apparent, not a word was said of the loss after the funeral. People couldn't talk about this person without getting emotional. So, no one did. Just the mention of the name would create tears. It would have taken a strong and courageous leader to lean into the pain instead of withdrawing from it. Just by one person's influence, I guarantee the healing process would have spread like wildfire through that congregation. That type of healing spreads like wildfire.

I can see the faces of the brave, loving people that helped me as I recall my journey of healing. As I think of these people, I am filled with so much appreciation and love. I pray that they are blessed beyond measure for loving a *broken me* through my heartbreak. All in the right timing they pointed my brokenness to God. This was especially true when I had those impossibly tough to answer questions.

Perhaps my most frequent prayer is that their love is so ingrained in me that I can't help but share with others that God puts in my life. I pray that I am strong enough to be the one who stands in love with those who are hurting.

Unfortunately, the advice and *help* of some people around us isn't so helpful. Often we find the *help* more of a stumbling block that seems to be just another obstacle in our journey of healing. This was true for the Israelites in their journey as well. The Israelites strength wasn't embraced well by the observers as well. We read in Ezra chapter 4:

> *"Then the peoples around them set out to discourage the people of Judah and make them afraid to go on building. They hired counselors to work against them and frustrate their plans during the entire reign of Cyrus king of Persia and down to the reign of Darius king of Persia." Ezra 4:4-5*

The same thing that happened to God's chosen people applies to us today as well. Often, it isn't when you are in a state of captivity, but that stage of finding freedom that will be threatening to some people. When you start throwing the shackles and chains off and seeing the light at the end of a tunnel, don't be surprised to find that the cheering dims to a faint whisper. For the Israelites, not only do the spectators try to discourage and instill fear in them, but they hired someone to complicate the Israelites' efforts. It was a personal vendetta to stop the progress of the Israelite people. We often demand in anger to know why someone would have the audacity to do something like that. We ask the same question all the time as we see the cruel injustices every day. The answer is, has been and always will be the same answer. The answer is Satan, and it happens because of his influence over people. He uses people as vessels to challenge God's people.

It was about six months after my accident. Shane and I had ordered pizza to be delivered and were casually watching T.V. in our living room as we impatiently waited for it. It was a lovely fall evening. We planned on a quiet evening, just the three of us. Everything went as planned until we got a knock on the door. My initial thought was "that was the fastest pizza delivery known to man, and I would be sure to throw a couple of extra dollars at him." As Shane answered the door, the response and discussion weren't what I would expect to go down with a pizza delivery man. The conversation was much too serious, and for some reason, Shane's voice seemed to be a little hushed. What I learned moments afterwards was that he was trying to be quiet so that I wouldn't hear the conversation being exchanged so that he may be the one to explain the situation to me. Out of curiosity, I walked up behind him to see a police officer handing him an envelope of papers.

What we received that day was another nightmare becoming my reality. We were being sued for the death of this man. Going from a person who had only had one statutory violation in her whole life (a minor in possession, which I don't think my parents know about to this day) to being sued wasn't something I was prepared to deal with. I remember opening the manila folder that contained the accusations that I could have done something differently that day to prevent it. They claimed I didn't hit my brakes hard enough or I that I should have veered harder to one side or another. This wasn't a new idea to me. Trust me when I say that I had already considered these *what if's* over and over. The problem was that I continually came up with the same answers. Most of the outcomes were that I could have killed someone else in all the other options and that it happened too fast to do anything differently. How badly I wished something else could have been done in the split instant.

The same family that I wanted to rush to and cry with was the family that wanted me to lose everything I had. They wanted me to pay for being in the exact place in the exact moment that ended their son's life. Truth be told, I didn't feel that they could break me any more than I was, not even if they took every possession I had. I would have been content at that moment to wander the streets aimlessly searching for hope. What kept me hanging on? Knowing I had to fight through it for my family.

Shortly after being served our papers, the pizza man arrived. Why did he arrive? Because you see life goes on. Life wasn't going to stop because this family blamed me. I could have cried and screamed that it wasn't fair, but it wasn't going to change my circumstances.

For the Israelites, being angry and mad wasn't going to change their situation either. It wasn't fair that they were trying to follow God after 70 years of captivity and the people around them cared only about complicating their progress. Life still went on for them, too. Yet we want, and often expect, to walk out of captivity into the world that embraces and loves us as we find healing. I wish we lived in a world like that, but then we wouldn't have any reason to long for Heaven, would we?

This is often one of the hardest lessons for us as we struggle in this world. The pain and agony we feel are often met with hatred, despised and with a lack of sympathy. It is hard for our finite mind to wrap itself around that fact. It was at this point for me that I learned how strong the powers against us really are. We can make light of Satan and his work until we are in this situation and the scriptures come alive in our lives. It is in those moments that we understand what Paul is telling the believers in Ephesus in Ephesians 6:12. During our struggle the Word of God comes alive:

> *"For our struggle is not against flesh and blood, but against the rulers, against the authorities, against the powers of this dark world and against the spiritual forces of evil in the heavenly realms"*

I know how it feels to not understand those words until there is a battle that has been waged and then they make all too much sense. It's the moments when there is a prize worth fighting for that we begin to understand the intensity and depth of the war that is waged over our souls.

Just as the temple the Israelites were building was worth fighting for, your soul is worth the fight. It wasn't the structure of the temple that created the threat for the Israelites. It isn't your mere existence that is a threat either. For the Israelites, the temple was a threat because of the deeper purpose that the building was to be used for. It would be a testimony of our God. It was a place that the people could show their dedication and love for the one true God. The temple was worth a fight. Let me remind you of Paul's words, "you are the temple." Your life can be a testimony of our God, and that is a fight worth fighting.

I remember questioning during this time in my life why it seemed like there were people against me. I was just trying to survive. I continually felt that I wasn't meeting the expectations and fulfilling the roles that people had put on my life. I was just trying to do the things God had asked of me not sink in the sinking sand of my sadness. I wonder as I read through Ezra if this is the same feeling the Israelites had. I wonder if they continually called out to God begging for protection from these outside influences so that they could faithfully follow God as they rebuilt the temple.

The problem for this world is that with God behind us we are a powerful force (Philippians 4:13). I'm not saying we are a wealthy force or a popular force, but a p-o-w-e-r-f-u-l, powerful force. We are powerful not because of what this earth gives, but what we give to this earth. We can give abundantly when it is coming straight to us from God. Therefore, for Satan to get at us, he is required to throw some low-ball punches to knock us down. That is exactly what happened with God's chosen as they rebuilt the temple.

I try to imagine the Israelite people busy at work. As they are faced with a rough task of building a temple, the people watching plot ways to disrupt them. If that doesn't get your blood boiling, you need to read back through the story again.

Several years after the Israelites began to build, those that opposed them were still trying to destroy their efforts. The next part of Ezra contains copies of letters sent from the adversaries of the Israelite people to the king, which at that time was King Xerxes, and later King Artaxerxes. The Israelite enemies claimed that the Jews were planning a rebellion. They were reminding the king in the letter of how rebellious this place was before, and that it was destroyed for a reason. They attempted to instill fear into the king to disrupt the building of the temple. I hate to tell you this, but for a moment it worked.

I don't know about you, but for me, this is exactly how my adversaries work. They want to dwell on my past mistakes. They want to remind me of my failures. They want to point out my sin as an excuse for not encouraging me to rebuild my life. Satan, my biggest adversary, reminds me of every reason why I should throw the towel in.

King Artaxerxes responds to the criticism with basically, "*You're so right, they have been rebellious in the past.*" He says that they dug up all the old records and did indeed find that these were rebellious people. I like how the New Living Translation says that these were indeed a "hotbed of insurrection against many kings" (Ezra 4:19). There are times in my life that I can recall being a *hotbed of rebellion.* I am so grateful that the state doesn't have records that they can pull up to remind me of these things (other than my minor in possession of course, but even that has been forgiven by now in the state of Utah).

If we were to carry a folder of failures with us, I would probably never be given a chance at anything. If every job interview meant that I would get my *records* pulled, I would be denied for being a *hotbed* every time. Satan does like to remind those around us of our failures. Through the blood of Jesus, we can look at our empty records and can have hope in a better future. Our records have been wiped clean. Thank you, Jesus!

King Artaxerxes orders that the Jews be stopped by force. The rebuilding of the temple was to be halted. Unfortunately, it wasn't suspended for a day or two, or even a couple of month. It was halted for 16 years.

God, however, never turned His back and never gave up on His children.

What happened next has God's name written all over it. Two men showed up, the prophet's Haggai and Zechariah. A movement to begin the rebuilding was led by Zerubbabel and Jeshua. As you can imagine the rebuilding resumed despite being questioned, doubted and harassed. Their adversaries wanted to know who gave them the authorization and who it was that was rebuilding. As if they were going to tattle-tale, they write a letter to the King, who at that particular time was King Darius. They write and tell him that the building has resumed and that they questioned the people who were responsible. They tell the King that, this is what the people rebuilding said:

> *"We are the servants of the God of heaven and earth, and we are rebuilding the temple that was built many years ago, one that a great king of Israel built and finished." Ezra 5:11*

They continue and flat out tell their junk to these people questioning them. "Yes, we were rebellious." "Yes, we were handed over to the Babylonians when we angered God." "Yes, our temple was destroyed." Then there comes the "but," "but we fought through, and we were told to rebuild." "Go dig up all of our junk and let us know what it is that you find." (My paraphrase of Ezra 5:11-17)

I love that passage. They own who they are. These people have endured to the point that they say, "Yes, that's who we are, and yes we are rebuilding this temple." That's when you know you have accepted the forgiveness.

The next letter is from King Darius, who digs in and finds the evidence of them being allowed to rebuild. So, he writes and says "do it!". Not only does he allow them to rebuild, but he returns all the articles that were stolen from the old Temple by the Babylonian army. Also, he covers the expenses of the workers as well as any of the animals needed for sacrifice. Not only does he allow it, but he also demands that anyone that tries to stop it will be impaled with a beam. Not any old beam, but it must be taken from their own home. (Ezra 6:3-12)

He signs the letter with this:

ANELL MELLISH*

> *"I Darius have decreed it. Let it be carried out with diligence" Ezra 6:12*

The NASB translation of the word *diligence* is that it is to be built fully, with great care. This word is used seven times between Ezra 5:8 and Ezra 7:26. Seven times in these letters, these people are said to be building diligently. They are building with great care. They are going to build that temple, and they will build it thoroughly, making sure each detail is done correctly.

Diligence, however, can be no match for this world, I hate to admit. We can be living productive lives, working hard for the right things and then walls can still come crashing down on us. Many times, the tragedy in our lives come at no fault to ourselves, but is collateral damage from the sin of others and can bring devastating loss. However, for the Israelites, the temple was torn down as a natural consequence of their own sin. Not all of them were guilty, though. For some, it was an unfair situation (some were marked on their foreheads (in Ezekiel) recognizing that they resisted idol worship and yet still had their temple torn down and thrown into captivity). I am sure that their cry was the same as ours, as we cry out about injustice and inequality. We must remind ourselves here of Paul's words when he says:

> *"If anyone destroys God's temple, God will destroy him; for God's temple is sacred, and you are that temple" 1 Corinthians 3:17*

We will be adversely affected by others sin. It's inevitable if we are in the world, fighting against the darkness of the world. It explains why Jesus tells that we must take up our cross *daily* and follow Him (Luke 9:23). There is nowhere to hide. It is the reason why people suffer abuse as children, get cheated on by a wandering spouse, abused by church clergy and all the other stories on the news that leave us with pure disgust and confusion.

So, the question comes down to how we are supposed to be living in such an unpredictable and cruel world? What will give us the strength and courage to leave what we know and look forward to what will be?

The dear friend of mine that I mentioned in the beginning that lost her son continues to choose to walk with courage and joy. There are so many things for her to mourn, but she has taken her life and dedicated the rebuilding of it to bring glory to the days that have passed. Her past doesn't stop her but spurs her on to living a bigger life. In fact, the miracle that I continually witness is that she lives a life that allows her son's life to continue to speak. It is an amazing sight to see, and yet that inexplicable joy and courage are there for all to seek and find.

PART TWO

CHAPTER FIVE

REBUILDING

Getting God Out of our "Box"

Why did the people rebuild as they were released from captivity? That answer is plain and simple; so that God would be honored. In the tabernacle and the temple, the glory of the Lord was present with the people. It was in the temple that they experienced the *Shekinah*, which means the dwelling of the Divine Presence of God.

In Exodus (Chapter 33) we get the chance to experience *Shekinah* through the eyes of Moses. We are told that Moses spoke with God as friends speak to one another. Moses asked God to teach him His ways and to guide him as a leader. Moses asked God what it was that would set them apart from everyone else. God clarified that it would be His presence that would make them unique. Moses had the favor of God. The next thing Moses said almost baffles me:

> *"Then Moses said, "Now show me Your Glory." Ex 33:18*

That was definitely a friend to friend comment. God agreed to let His entire goodness pass in front of Moses but told Moses that he couldn't look at His face because no one could see His face and still live. God instructed Moses to hide in a cleft of the rock, and after His presence passed, Moses would see His back. In Chapter 34, we are told that Moses' face was radiant from speaking with God, and he would cover his face with a veil. His face was so radiant that the people were afraid of him. Now that is some kind of *Shekinah*.

When Moses was done building the tabernacle, the Glory of the Lord filled the place and was so strong that Moses couldn't enter. Later, as they offered sacrifices, the Glory of the Lord appeared to all the people as it consumed the sacrifice. The people's response to witnessing such a sight was to shout for joy and fall facedown. In the Book of Numbers, as the people rebelled, the Glory of the Lord appeared, and each time it caused the people to fall facedown. Have you ever experienced something that was so powerful that it causes you to fall facedown? The overwhelming emotion of the presence of God is unique in the fact that it can cause the strongest of men to fall on their faces.

We again see the Shekinah when Solomon completed the temple. In 1 Kings, Chapter 8 we read that the Glory of the Lord filled the temple, and was such a powerful force that the priests were unable to perform their duties. Again, in 2 Chronicles, as Solomon offered the sacrifices, the Glory of the Lord consumed them. The Word tells us that what the people witnessed standing outside was fire coming down, and the Glory of the Lord was above the temple. What was their reaction? It brought them to their knees, and their faces to the ground. Worship and thanksgiving followed. We are told that as they worshipped they were saying, "He is good, His love endures forever."

I try to grasp the emotions they must have felt. I think of the most amazing thing my eyes have witnessed and still struggle to wrap my mind around this magnitude of glory. I imagine my kids' eyes as they watch fireworks. When they were young, the magnitude of the fireworks was overwhelming to them. Each blast would scare one of them to tears. They didn't understand why we would be so enthralled with such loud, scary noises. As they grew and began to understand colors and the uniqueness of the fireworks, they started appreciating them. If you sit with a group of people watching fireworks, though, there is a universal response that happens. You get an "*ooohh, ahhhh*" response as people stare into the heavens and appreciate the splendor of the moment.

The fire that rained down from the heavens, witnessed by the Israelites must have been so much more awesome. Not only did it get the "*ooohh, ahhhh*" response, but it was so powerful that it drove every one of those people to their knees. I like Strong's

Concordance example of the word *worship*, to go prostate, especially reflexive, in homage to God. Reflexive, meaning this was the immediate response to the Glory of God. It didn't need to be taught or explained. Shekinah brings people to their knees.

When the exiles returned to rebuild the temple, there was no moment where they witnessed the Shekinah. They don't see a cloud return, and the temple isn't filled with the Spirit. After 22 years of building, they dedicate the temple, they do it with joy. Just as they did for the tabernacle and Solomon's temples, they make their offering, but unlike those other occasions, no fire comes down and consumes the offerings. There is no Shekinah as described in the earlier days of the temple. When Ezra and the exiles that return with him returned and made offerings, again we saw no evidence of the Glory of the Lord. As I read the Word, I feel as if something is missing. There is no falling on their faces as they acknowledge how good our God is, nor any worship recorded. No fire comes down to devour the offerings. Did Ezra forget to mention that? Surely not, and for 400 years they wait.

At the beginning of the New Testament, the Glory of the Lord appears to some shepherds, and we are told that they were terrified. The angel appears and tells them do not be afraid, that their Savior was born. We are told that the Heavenly Hosts appeared and began praising God saying "Glory to God in the highest." Do you feel the same sense of hope, happiness, and joy that I do? We know that this little Savior grows up to be the Son of God, who dies on the cross for all our sins, creating a new covenant with God. Matthew records that at the same moment that Jesus cried out and gave up His spirit, the curtain in the temple was torn in two. The curtain that separated us from the Holy of Holies, the spot where the presence of God was to reside was torn. Make no mistake that there was no more need for the curtain in the temple.

This game changing gift that was promised by Isaiah and Jeremiah comes in the book of Acts, Chapter 2:

> *"Suddenly a sound like the blowing of a violent wind came from heaven and filled the whole house where they were sitting. They saw what*

seemed to be tongues of fire that separated and came to rest on each of them. All of them were filled with the Holy Spirit and began to speak in other tongues as the Spirit enabled them"
Acts 2:2-4

This was the gift to the believers of that day, and every believer since. The day Jesus died, the curtain was torn, the Spirit was given to each believer, and now *we* are the temple. We are the holy place where the Spirit of God resides. We are the sacred, beloved, righteous temples of God.

I wish that we would acknowledge the impact of what happens when a person submits their life to God. Maybe if the Spirit came through blowing a violent wind, looking like tongues of fire, we would truly appreciate the impact of the moment.

I don't remember a blowing of the wind as I was filled with the Spirit at an early age. I was nine-years-old, had just lost my Pappaw and, through my broken heart, I gave God all I had and was filled with His Spirit. What an awesome, incredible moment! It was a gift, an eternal gift. It was a gift beyond any other and had a deeper impact than any other in my life that I have made or ever will make. It was the gift that set me apart and marked my life to be one following God. Let me clarify that this gift never guaranteed a life of ease. What it guaranteed me was a life of love. It is a gift of love beyond measure.

Those of us who experience tragedy of any sort often ask the same question. We wonder, "If we are following God, why wouldn't He protect me?" So, why would we try to rebuild? We will restore our temples for the same reason the Jews rebuilt the Temple. We follow Him through a journey of recovery so that our God may be honored. It is through Him we find the strength, the materials and the place to rebuild. Everything we need to get through our trials, struggles, fear, doubts and worries, He will provide. He knows what we need. It's the blessing of being a child of God. We aren't required to carry the burden alone.

What I find interesting about my accident, is I can remember thinking at an earlier age that I just wouldn't be able to live with myself if I ever killed a person. If I ever hit someone with my vehicle, I knew I wouldn't be able to cope with the emotions. The burden seemed beyond what I was humanly able to carry. It is what I can call, *my worst nightmare*. On May 9, 2007, I lived through it. There were days that I probably didn't want to live through it or didn't know how to live through it, but here I am, nine years later. *I lived through it.* Today, I look at my kids and wonder how I would live through losing one of them as my friend did when she lost her son. But I'm reminded that I wouldn't do it alone. If such a tragedy lay in my future, I know God would walk me through it, one step at a time. He would supply me with the materials I needed to rebuild exactly as He wanted. I will make it through anything with Him, even the things that make my heart instantly break just thinking about them.

As a believer, our temples must be rebuilt. We must be Shekinah for the rest of the world. Sometimes the walk we take just to survive speaks more than any evangelism tactics of our day. When we are stuck in a state of suffering, we look to the Word of God and realize that we aren't alone. Sometimes knowing that bad things happen, and they happen to all sorts of people, can help. We see the words that God spoke into scripture to carry us through and help us realize that He created us to overcome all sorts of obstacles, hand in hand with Him.

Before the fall of Jerusalem, the ruler of the land was King Zedekiah. We are told that he was only 21-years-old when he first became king and ruled a total of eleven years, making him 32-years-old. I'm 32 as of the writing of this book. I look at all the mistakes I've made in the last eleven years and realize that I stand on no premise to judge the bad decision Zedekiah made. We are told that he did just as much evil as the generations before him in the Lord's eyes. Zedekiah provoked the Babylonians into the action that the prophets had been warning of. The city was under siege, experienced severe famine, and eventually was overtaken by the Babylonian army. The king fled the city and was finally captured. He was taken to Babylon, and the Word tells us, that in front of his own eyes, the Babylonians not only killed his sons but slaughtered them. It was the last sight that Zedekiah saw, as they put out his eyes, and threw him in prison until the day that he died.

I know what you are probably thinking of the story of this king. Natural consequences to his sin resulted in a disastrous outcome. For some of us, this may be the same situation. We are so deep in sin that it requires an enormous fall for God to rebuild our temples in the manner that He needs. Some of us may look at this as punishment, but years after the incident, it will look as if God saved us. The fall pulls us out of death's grip of sin and replaces it with love so true that it lasts an eternity. King Zedekiah was even warned repeatedly of the imminent doom that would be brought on by the Babylonians. In fact, Jeremiah records a conversation where he explicitly warned the king with the exact details of what would happen. The king made several excuses as to why he wasn't going to listen. It was his fear of what would happen that prevented him having faith.

Sometimes, our temples are torn down, not because of sin, but because of the sins of others. The prophet Jeremiah knew what it required to serve God through unfair and challenging circumstances. Jeremiah was called at a young age to be a prophet for God, and throughout his life he watched sin run rampant throughout the nation. He then witnessed the siege by the Babylonian army. The Book of Jeremiah gives us an account of his pleas to the people to turn from their sinful ways and the consequences that would follow if they didn't heed God's will. He pleads with King Zedekiah to listen and avoid the devastation to follow.

In Jeremiah Chapter 39, we are told that all the people were taken captives. The only ones left behind were the poor people who owned nothing. These were probably the people that were deemed useless by the Babylonians. Jeremiah was left behind with the others. He experienced heartache, failure, and devastation due to the hardened hearts of those that caused the fall.

We can sit back and wonder how *fair* Jeremiah's situation was. We can claim that it's not fair for one person's sin to affect another. We can cry in anguish and offense to God that we were doing everything that we were supposed to be doing and it's not fair. This was my cry to God in 2007, as I lay awake at night wondering why I had to be eternally changed by the decisions of a stranger.

When Shane and I were married in 2005, I was a drill sergeant in the Air Force. My career was exciting and life changing. Every six weeks I would walk a flight of 50 or so young men down a walkway that marked the entrance into the United States Air Force. During those six weeks, I would pour my heart and soul into changing their life. Many needed to be totally broken down to be built back up. Shane and I married, and I was looking forward to a long and successful career in the military that would indeed require some sacrifice. I was willing to lay it all on the line. That is until about six weeks after we returned from our Jamaican honeymoon when I discovered I was pregnant. It changed my whole path. I knew that I could never ask the amount of sacrifice that would be required from a family with two military spouses. I gave up the one thing that made me feel like I was touching lives around me.

After separating from the military in February, only a few short weeks before I had my daughter, I was focused on finishing up my degree and doing the best that I could with the situation I was in. I was focused, motivated and trying to maintain a relationship with God. May 9th was never in my plan. I didn't believe it was fair that God would require such sacrifice from me when I thought I was giving my best to Him. There were moments of weakness that I remember demanding to know *why*. *Why* would He do this to me? *Why* couldn't He have me leave ten seconds later then it wouldn't have been my car, but that of the one in front of me? He could have had my college final scheduled for ten minutes before or after, and again, it wouldn't have been my car. He could have cleared the interstate for that minute it would have taken for the man to run across all eight lanes to get where he was going. God could have prevented the collision between my life and that man's, but He didn't. He didn't protect me that morning from the tragedy I was about to face.

So back to our arguments about fairness, it wasn't fair. Why would He pick me? In the midst of my outburst on fairness, I am reminded of the words that the prophet Isaiah foretold to the people of Judah.

> *"Surely he took up our infirmities and carried our sorrows, yet we considered him stricken by God, smitten by him, and afflicted. But he was pierced for our transgressions, he was crushed for our iniquities; the punishment that brought us peace was upon him, and by his wounds we are healed. We all, like sheep, have gone astray, each of us has turned his own way; and the Lord has laid on him the iniquity of us all."*
> *Isaiah 53:4-6*

And with that, our complaint of *fairness* looks irrelevant. Isaiah was telling the people that there would be a day that all their sins would be taken away, that someone was going to pay the price for their sin. So, life is unfair but not as unfair as Jesus' death.

This argument then brings us to what? We get through watching the day that our temples are destroyed, and then we look in the mirror and have no idea what is to come but, we remember what we used to be. Whether we were deep in the sin that caused us to fall, or it came out of nowhere with no reason, we still wonder what we are to do next?

Psalm 137 tells us what the exiles did while they were in Babylon. They sat and wept. Weeping in the manner described at the reuniting of long lost loved ones (Genesis 33:4), and a loving embrace of a forgiven relative for their terrible sin toward another (Genesis 45:14). In this same way, we weep at the burial sight of a loved one, these people wept (2 Samuel 3:32). This weeping was not the frustrated tears from a bad day, but the gut wrenching, heart break weeping. The exiles wept as they remembered their home.

The day they held the funeral for the man that I hit (that still hurts to say), I wanted to go. I wanted to pay my respect to the family, but I knew in my gut that the last person they would want to see was the person that they stood accusing. I had to do something, so with my husband and three of my closest friends, we drove down to the place of the accident with our lovely spring flowers and stood in a circle and prayed to God. A friend of mine said a prayer that told God we didn't understand any of this, but we prayed for His strength and understanding, and that the family would find peace. It seemed like we had an itty-bitty flashlight in a pitch-black hole trying to find our way out. I placed flowers on the spot where the man died, and I sat there, crouched down, holding the flowers, and I wept. I can remember saying I didn't want to leave because I didn't want it to be true. Clinging to the flowers made it seem unreal until I acknowledged it was true and let go of the flowers.

Years later, I stopped by to speak to the man from the auto body shop who witnessed the accident. I didn't know his name, but I remembered him. I walked into the shop and asked the person behind the desk for the man that was working when someone got hit by a car on the highway. They walked into the garage, and I thought it was a long shot that anyone would remember me. Within a moment that man walked through the doors and ran straight over to me and welcomed me with an unexpected embrace. He expressed how happy he was to see me, and I tried to put words to the gratitude that I had in my heart. He told me of seeing us standing out there praying, and how terrible he felt for me, how it absolutely broke his heart, and how he often wondered about me. I never would have thought anyone cared about me as I stood on the side of the highway clutching those flowers, not knowing how to let go.

On my weak days, I was a shell. On my strong days, I wept. The more I wept, the more love I felt. I wonder, as the exiles sat by the river in an unknown and foreign land and wept, how abundantly God loved them at that moment?

The probability of some of you reading this and being shut down to such an emotional plea is high. Therefore, I am going to be bold in my next statement. If you think it is ridiculous that you need to weep in such a moment and are thinking thoughts such as *just move on*, then I am going to caution you. The reason for that is either you don't understand tragedy or your heart is hardened to brokenness. Throughout my journey, I have experienced so many people that would like to see me ignore any pain and tell them how wonderful I am. There were times I would try to do that, but instead of making everything wonderful it made me feel as though I was suffocating. In fact, at one point I felt the world had grown dark, and I was trying to just get enough air to breath. After talking to a deeply loved mentor, she asked me what my family thought of what I was going through. I told her I wasn't telling them because I didn't want them to worry. She then explained *co-dependency* to me, and I realized I was trying to bear my pain alone by shutting everyone out.

David, also known as the man after God's own heart, was a griever. When he learned of Saul's death, we are told in 2 Samuel 1:11 that David responded by tearing his clothes, mourning, weeping, and fasting. If you remember, Saul was trying to kill David, and yet David still responded in such a manner. After Absalom, David's son killed Amnon for raping his sister, Tamar, we read in 2 Samuel 13:31 that David laid on the ground and tore his clothes. We see this type of mourning all throughout the Bible. Job mourned the death of his sons by shaving his head and falling to the ground in worship, obviously in a humbled state of mind as he clung to the only hope he knew. Jacob mourned the loss of his sons by tearing his clothes, and the Word says he mourned for many days.

The statistics for the number of rapes that go unreported is startling. We handle sexual abuse today by hiding it and directing the blame inward. In the Old Testament, we see that it was dealt with by mourning. Tamar was raped by her brother, and we read that she responded by tearing her garment that was meant for virgin royalty and put ashes on her forehead. As she walked away from her rapist, she doesn't hide or shove all her emotions down. No, Tamar walked away *weeping* as she went. She responded in a way that announced to the world what just happened.

The strongest, most courageous, holiest man that I know wept. In the New Testament, when Jesus' friend Lazarus died, he met with Mary and the people with her. The group of people was all weeping, and we are told that Jesus told them to *toughen up*. That isn't true. Jesus was "deeply moved in spirit and troubled" and then "Jesus wept." Jesus raised Lazarus from the dead, but at the sight of his dearly loved friend Mary weeping, it brought him to tears. The Jews that witnessed Jesus weeping said: "See how He loved him!" (John 11:33-36).

When did weeping as a response to heartbreak become unacceptable? Why don't we think it is acceptable to weep with each other? At the time of my weeping, I remember people who came and wept with me. There was nothing more healing or more comforting than someone offering their humble hearts as an offering of their love for me. Just as Jesus' weeping showed His love for the people, it shows our love for each other.

At the sight of sin, Jesus weeps. Instead of gossiping and being critical, He weeps. In Luke Chapter 19, as He approached Jerusalem, He looked over it and wept. He then said, "If you, even you, had only known on this day what would bring you peace -

but now it is hidden from your eyes." Loving those who are in the midst of their sin doesn't look like ignoring them. It means being saddened by the victory of sin over someone and being honest with them.

If we are striving to be like Jesus more and more every day, then we need to be able to weep for the circumstances in life that breaks our hearts. Man, woman and child can invest in each other, and accept the tears that others shed as an act of drawing close to God in the unity of one spirit. In fact, Paul gives us instructions how to love each other, and he says we are to:

> *"Rejoice with those who rejoice; mourn with those who mourn" Romans 12:15*

If you struggle with grief, sorrow, mourning, and weeping you are missing out on seeing a love that unites instead of divides. Not only are you missing out on an opportunity to be blessed, but you are also leaving those who are broken to struggle on their own. I believe that weeping doesn't mean that we are all called to sit down and cry. Not all of us are gifted in that way. For some of us, mourning means serving that person. It's why so many of us start cooking a meal for people who are going through hard times. For some of us, mourning with another person means praying for another. Prayer warriors will dive into praying for another person when that person has no words to offer to God. What a blessing. For others, mourning may mean giving guidance, spiritual direction, our presence, etc. And for some of us, mourning does mean sitting down, holding the hand of a neighbor and crying with them. If you are curious of a Christian's gifting, it becomes apparent in the midst of tragedy.

We don't see Jesus tell Mary that everything will be okay. He doesn't have the *right* words to say to Mary or answer all her questions why. He just shows that He loves her, and I guarantee that was enough. It takes a strong believer to weep with someone who is hurting, no matter what *weeping* looks like.

This isn't to say that we must sit around crying 24 hours a day. What else are we supposed to do during our brokenness? The prophet Jeremiah gave us good advice in the letter he wrote to the exiles in Babylon. He told them to build houses and settle down, plant gardens, marry, have families, seek peace and prosperity of Babylon, and pray. These are simple priorities, yet crucial in bringing us healing. My answer was very similar in those minutes of weeping, asking God what am I supposed to do now. He responded that I was to love my baby, love my husband, make a home that is a safe place, pray for that man's family, seek peace, and seek forgiveness for my sins. The answer was as simple for me as it was for the exiles; search for the things that bring you a smile. Don't attempt to escape your situation.

As we weep and search for the things that bring us peace, we recall the words of the prophets during the Babylonian exile from God, "Return to me, and I will return to you."

CHAPTER SIX

TAKE IT TO THE ALTAR!

Realizing All We Have to Give is Our Heart

    I credit so much of my healing to a recovery program called, *Celebrate Recovery* written by John Baker. I began the 12-Step process claiming that I was perfectly fine. In my cold and shut down soul I was thoroughly convinced that I didn't need recovery from anything. The only reason I would go was to *support my **messed-up** friends.* I had the *"my life is wonderful"* attitude. The truth is I began to believe that lie to prevent my heart from bearing the weight of acknowledging my hurts, bad habits, and awful hang-ups. I opened the book and read the first chapter title, **Denial**. It meant nothing to me at first, and it is only by the grace of God that I slowly began to feel the weight of the tremendous sorrow that burdened my soul, and I realized how disturbed I was. It hit me like a ton of bricks. How is it possible to go from being ***perfect*** to feeling like such a wreck? I realized that I had nothing to offer, that my sins were too hard to bear for me, and that all I could offer God was my heart.

*That was **exactly** what He was waiting for.*

The book of Ezra takes us step-by-step through the process of rebuilding the temple. In Chapter 2, Ezra tells us that the brave souls who went back equaled 42,360 people. When they arrived, they settled down in their old towns. As a military family, I understand what *settling down* means. The Israelites found a place to live and brought their donkeys in with the items they owned. Then they unpack their belongings into a new dwelling that they now called *home*. I realize that a donkey would never cut it for us today, and it's a bigger ordeal for us as we waited for the moving trucks to arrive. After seeing our boxes of household items, a donkey seemed appealing and a much simpler process that I truly longed for.

After they had settled in their homes, they came together as *one* and said, *"Now what?"* (My paraphrasing of Ezra 3:1). What they built first surprised me, but they built an altar. There are no temple walls up yet, no port-a-potties for the workers (all kidding aside). There was nothing but the altar.

"Then Jeshua son of Jozadak and his fellow priests and Zerubbabel son of Shealtiel and his associates began to build the altar of the God of Israel to what is written in the Law of Moses the man of God. Despite their fear of the peoples around them, they built the altar on its foundation and sacrificed burnt offerings on it to the Lord, both morning and evening sacrifices ...On the first day of the seventh month they began to offer burnt offerings to the Lord, though the foundation of the Lord's temple had not yet been laid" Ezra 3:2-6

If you have a curious mind such as I do, you may be wondering why they would build the altar first.

The answer to that should provide us a road map on our journey as well.

There is so much information listed in the Bible about the exact sacrifices and offerings that were made in specific situations. I will hesitantly admit I generally skim over those verses. I've missed the significance of the words in those chapters. When we glide past the significance of what the inspired Word of God is telling us, we miss pieces of what is happening.

In the Old Testament, it was a process to be in right standing with God. Dedication to God required service from His people. Gratitude is normally the feeling I experience as I read the work these people had to go through to have their sins forgiven. The sacrificial Lamb of God, who died over 2,000 years ago, took the work off my hands, and so I am reminded of my profound gratitude.

However, for the Israelites, the offerings and sacrifices meant something. The altar was a big part of the tabernacle and the temple. It was at the altar that the people pledged their love and dedication to God who had brought them through the incredible story of the Old Testament.

The people brought their offerings, and God accepted them. In this beautiful exchange, the people recognized that God is sovereign, and God approved of His people. The significance of the altar is lost on us today as we don't need an altar. The beautiful exchange was Jesus' life.

We realize the Israelites weren't robots. They were a slice of the human population. They represented all of us who struggle with issues that prevent us from bringing an offering to God. They represented those of us who hide our hearts from God, in fear that it will never be enough. They represented those of us who turn away from a relationship with Him due to a complete lack of self-love.

Just as I lived in a land of denial before my car accident, many of us have no idea the status of our hearts. Some claim to love God, and are going to church, but walk an entirely different walk when the church isn't watching. We focus more on what we can give to a church rather than the pure offering of our heart to God. On the altar, we place our possessions, our deeds, and our attendance records. All this is worthless in the beautiful exchange.

Our hearts aren't generally disobedient for fun, though. The struggles of this world aren't black and white. There is a land that is commonly described in the Old Testament, that if we could visualize it, would have an old wooden sign in front of it marked with the word **BEWARE**. This land was used as an illustration that the people of those days understood. It was commonly used to describe a soul that was without God. This land, which the Prophets Isaiah and Jeremiah described often, is a land of jackals. This isn't something that we are familiar with today, but for the Israelites, they would have understood this analogy. Land that is filled with jackals is land that is deserted by humans; a land that is void of human activity. Translations of the word *jackal* give us insight that these jackals aren't a good sign. One such translation gives us dragons, monsters, serpents that haunt a land that was once inhabited and is now deserted. Jeremiah warns in Chapter 9, Verse 11:

"I will make Jerusalem a heap of ruins, a haunt of Jackals; and I will lay waste the towns of Judah so no one can live there."

Has your heart and soul become a desolate land that is haunted by jackals? Why does this happen? Jeremiah tells us that the Lord says this happens because we turn from His ways and follow the stubbornness of our hearts and other gods (Jeremiah 9:11-14). We put other things on our altar and measure our goodness in *earthly* terms. Slowly our souls turn from God and resemble a land of jackals.

Mass and public shootings have become so commonplace that I find myself becoming apathetic to the reality and tragedy of what has happened. Kids killing kids, soldiers killing soldiers, one parent killing the other, and terrorist attacks have become daily news. We wonder what has possibly happened to a person's heart that they are willing to shed innocent blood. Even the blood of the young, the innocent, and the loved are innocently slain. I'm not naive enough to believe that on a pleasant morning, a man decided to go into a school and shoot innocent children because he was so overly content and filled with an incredible spirit of love. I can't see the true spirit of his soul, but I can only imagine the land has become a desolate land, haunted by jackals, by the serpent that fights to overcome our victory and triumphs through sin. While so many people point the blame toward guns, we must recognize the deficiency in a soul that is the actual cause.

Our soul doesn't become a land of jackals overnight. It happens one day when we decide to put some *thing* before God. The next day, we forget to pray. The next day, we decide we can *do* life on our own. The next day, we see an easy and quick opportunity and fall into sin. It's a slippery slope that ends in heartache and disaster, and it is by the grace of God that we don't end up as a land of jackals.

The living, breathing, Word of God is very specific in cautioning us about the problems that we all will face. These signs of caution apply to us just as to the Israelites who were tempted. Jeremiah Chapter 9 identifies two of these problems that we should be cautious of.

Stubborn Hearts

The first is the stubbornness of hearts. This word *stubbornness* is also translated into lustful, imaginations of the heart. So, what does it truly mean to have a stubborn, imaginative, lustful heart? The Bible warns us throughout that a prideful heart is to be feared.

A prideful heart is perhaps the most common and deceptive condition that holds us back from the love of the Father. There is a condition of the human race that is a common theme throughout the Bible and is quoted throughout the Old and New Testaments. This condition is when people have eyes, but cannot see... have ears, but do not hear. Why would we have ears and eyes, but not be able to hear or see? The answer is we chose our own sinful and evil desires over the will of God. Paul writes in the Book of Romans that this is also a "spirit of stupor" (Romans 11:8). We believe *we* know better than Him, and so we choose to do things our own way.

The Apostle Peter tells us that being nearsighted and blind results from forgetting that we have been cleansed of our sin (2 Peter 1:9). Self-centeredness, pride, and forgetfulness are some of the conditions that we bear witness to with the Israelites. They forgot that God rescued their ancestors from cruel, Egyptian slavery. They forgot He brought them through the desert and gave them the land that was promised to them. They forgot the daily provisions of quail and manna. They forgot the miracle parting of the Red Sea. They began worrying about themselves, in the here and now.

After studying about jackals, this is going to sting a bit, but Jeremiah says:

> *"Even Jackals offer their breasts to nurse their young, but my people have become heartless like ostriches in the desert" Lamentations 4:3*

Job warns of these *ostriches* because of the self-centeredness of an ostrich. They will leave their eggs in the hot sun, and forget about them, and at times even crush their own eggs because of their forgetfulness. Not only are these people jackals, but they have become prideful, forgetful, selfish people. The hardships that they have endured haven't made them stronger. It hasn't brought them perseverance that leads to godliness (2 Peter 1:6) but instead turned them inward to their selfishness.

The fork in the road looks like this; turn upward to God through hardship, which will lead outward as you reflect the Glory of God. Or, turn inward, toward your selfish, sinful desires, and you will become a person who has ears and eyes, but neither hears nor sees. You will become a person out for yourself and will care little about the suffering of others. You will throw your possessions and deeds on the altar, and expect God to meet you there. Peter tells us that ultimately if we become this type of person, we will be ineffective and unproductive for God.

One path leads to corruption and evil, the other leads to "a rich welcome into the eternal kingdom of our Lord and Savior Jesus Christ" (2 Peter 1:11). Seeing the clear path that is the *right* one, and choosing it can be two entirely different things, though. Knowing that many chose the path of a prideful heart is a frightening thought. We live amongst people that have ears and eyes but aren't hearing or seeing.

This is what I experienced through recovering from my accident. People saw me struggling with their eyes, but they didn't see the bigger picture of the battle, and the mountain that I was climbing. They heard the words that came out of my mouth but didn't understand the brokenness behind them. What they would see and hear was a person that was weaker than them, and in a place of devastation, and for some reason that gave them a reason to judge. For a while, I wasn't a *fun* person to be around, and that seemed to be awfully disturbing to most people's schedule.

As for me, I had a choice to make. I could forget that the accident took the life of a man that fateful morning. I could forget that he had a mother and family that were at home grieving, and if I forgot that they existed, then I would be *free and clear* to continue with my life. I could be mad at him for walking out onto an eight-lane interstate. I could blame him for drinking so heavily at ten in the morning. I could tell everyone that asked me that it was his fault and that for me it was just a freak accident. I could make assumptions about some of my own questions, and tell people that he was committing suicide. I could make myself pick this path of selfishness that put a reason and answer behind everything to justify a heartless reaction. I can tell you it would have been easier than to walk through the brokenness.

Overcoming this pathway is to follow in the same plea that we read in Lamentations:

"Restore us to yourself, O Lord, that we may return; renew our days as of old" *Lamentations 5:21*

This is a path of brokenness, as we open our eyes and hand our hearts over to God. In our brokenness, we place our hearts in a million pieces on the altar.

For me to accept my broken heart, I had to face all the brokenness of the situation. I had to acknowledge that a mom was grieving the loss of her son. I know she probably remembered the day she gave birth to him like I had experienced five short weeks earlier. I had to step out of my selfishness and realize I didn't have all the answers, and that it wasn't going to make sense. This pathway seemed harder, especially for the strong-willed person that I am. Following this path meant to be broken, and accept that we don't know what our tomorrow holds. Our hope comes from leaning on the One who does know. We humbly hand our life and heart over to Him and ask for His strength and love as we struggle through trying times. These times that no one in this world can see or understand.

When you choose the pathway of crying out to God, it may *initially* feel like you are lost. It's part of acknowledging the pain. This pain will be comparable to a thirst in your soul that only God can fill. Your own evil and sinful desires will leave you feeling unsatisfied, as they hold no water to quench your thirst.

This thirst will bring you to your knees and, will eventually lead you to turn upward as your cries bring Glory to God. You see people in your life that you never planned on or expected as beautiful gifts from God. You realize that two years before the accident, as you were spending your time drinking and having a big party, God was putting the puzzle pieces in place for that fateful day. He does this because He loves you, and knows what your tomorrow holds.

I found myself clinging to my daughter tightly for the next several days. She was only five-weeks old, and whenever the panic and fear would sweep over me, I would look at her precious face sleeping and realize that there is a God, that He is not dead, and that He's got this. Her precious little face would reflect a love much greater than anything on this earth. As I submitted to this pathway, I realized that there was a hierarchy on this planet and that no one could be at the top other than God. I would cry to Shane, asking him why this happened, and more than once he would just shake his head having no idea what to say. The strongest man I knew and who loves me most in this world couldn't answer my questions. Only God could.

My answer to one of the hardest questions came months after the accident. I cried out to God, "*Why* would you pick me that day when you could have veered either one of us off that exact schedule, and it wouldn't have been me?". My answer was the man that I hit had a destiny that had nothing to do with me. I wasn't going to understand the circumstances or the life this man was leading. I wasn't going to know if he was trying to cross the interstate or if he was indeed committing suicide to end his life. I would know nothing until I sat face to face with Jesus and then He would answer all my questions. Jesus would give me truth on that day. The question for me became whether I was willing to wait for the truth or not? I am, and I still long for that day when all the answers are clear to me. I realized that day that if my path had nothing to do with the man's that I hit, then I had to believe that God had chosen me that day. That is such a harsh reality if you decide to believe that God is good. I didn't know why, but there was a reason, and

I had to trust God's judgment. If He picked me, then He knew that I was capable of getting through it. I didn't know how, but I had to be willing to follow Him through the wilderness.

Stubborn hearts can also be due to greed so deeply rooted in a person's soul that they refuse to acknowledge God's truth. We struggle with the same issue today that the Israelites struggled with. Jeremiah tells us in Ezekiel that the Israelites would put God in a box and ask Him to be whatever they needed on their own agenda. Sound familiar?

"With their mouths they express devotion, but their hearts are greedy for unjust gain. Indeed, to them you are nothing more than one who sings love songs with a beautiful voice and plays an instrument well, for they hear your words but do not put them into practice"
Ezekiel 33:31-32

Our churches are filled with these people still today, and we are all guilty of this at some level. We praise the God of ultimate grace and mercy on Sunday mornings, and on our way out of the church parking lot we are willing to run each other over to get out first. We want to take the grace, but keep control of our own lives. All of this in a desperate attempt to live a life of our own accord, and chase the false security of control. We pick through what we want to take from God, and our stubborn hearts hang on to what seems comfortable.

What takes place in our churches that drive many Christ followers to turn away is appalling. God is in fact not just a God that sings of His love, He is the God of heaven and earth. He is the God that rules each moment of every day of the lives of every creature that roams this earth. His love is grander than we can imagine and His authority isn't limited by our agenda. Living this pathway of putting God in our box will end in devastation as we miss out on the fullness of God.

This land of jackals is marked with a ***BEWARE*** sign for a reason. We are surrounded by a lackluster, half-hearted type of dedication to God in our society. We are warned for a reason. It will be a fight for the truth. This battle won't be glamourous by society's terms.

We are often convinced that living a life dedicated to God isn't a victory. Society will look at the narrow path and notice how hard and unglamorous it looks. They don't understand the ultimate prize or the eternal promise. Ezekiel, a priest of the time, was in exile in Babylon at this time. The reassurance that the Lord offers to him still applies to us today:

> *"Son of man, you are living among a rebellious people. They have eyes to see but do not see and ears to hear but do not hear, for they are a rebellious people" Ezekiel 12:2*

Instead of dismissing Ezekiel to simply blend in with the nation, God asked him to stand out. He asked him to be a sign that God was working through him, as a reminder to the people that God still reigns.

The Bible is full of people that stand out, and we repeatedly read of the strength it takes to be able to walk this path. It's why in the New Testament, Paul reminds us that we can do ***ALL*** things through Christ, who gives us strength (Philippians 4:13). He does the same for you and me.

As we find ourselves misunderstood by the people around us, we must remember that God calls us to be strong for Him, to stand up against injustice and rebellion. It will be a lonely and scary road at times. We aren't alone, though. Jeremiah faced this same sense of fear as he watched the people turn against God and do as they wished. Reading his words, make no mistake of the tremendous struggle he faced, but God is not like us. God doesn't shut us out or turn his ears and eyes away. He is always with us. Just read Jeremiah's words:

> *"I called on your name, O Lord from the depths of the pit. You heard my plea; "do not close your ears to my cry for relief". You came near when I called you and you said, "Do not fear". Lamentations 3:55-57*

Jeremiah's story is marked with heartbreak and pain. He begged God to pay the people back for their plots, insults, and mocking. I don't know about you, but I can relate to that sort of anger, yet we are called to live a life of forgiveness. I wish I could say that takes the heartbreak away from what we experienced, but sadly it doesn't. The promise for us all is the same promise Jeremiah received, ***Do Not Fear***.

Often tragedy brings you to your knees in ways that result in a dramatic change in the way you live. God will sweep down in your most desperate hour and cradle you in ***His loving arms***. The devotion you will feel from these moments will strike a match to the love of God that most resembles gas-soaked wood just waiting for a match. We all have the potential for unbridled passion, but tragedy will have us laying our hearts on the altar due to the desperation we experience in an almost frantic manner. Those around you won't understand this sort of dedication and commitment to our God. And yet, this is precisely what He wants from us.

I found myself pleading with God, how was I supposed to carry on my life, while the man that I hit that morning couldn't. The answer came in the sweetest, safest answer as He said, "You live bigger and better for him." That answer took away all my selfishness and replaced it with a reason bigger than myself, and it's big enough not to let anyone stop me. What I have painfully found out is, even Christ followers are threatened by that drive in me because it takes the control that they want in my life away. For that, I must continually look to God with my plea and cry for help. Would you believe my answer repeatedly is, ***Do Not Fear***?

Giving our Hearts to Idols

The second pathway that Jeremiah warns to avoid becoming a land of jackals is by putting other gods before God, the Father. It was due to their fear that the Israelites were worshipping other gods.

In the same way, we have a pathway to pick. One path is that which promises love, grace, mercy, strength, and endurance unlike anything else on this planet.

The other pathway promises all that too, but can't deliver on any of the promises. They are all *empty* promises that will give you something to hope for, but nothing to hold on to. Other gods are deceiving, manipulative and not always so obvious.

The temptation we face to follow the quick answer of false gods is no surprise to God. He warns us through Jeremiah that we should be appalled at idol worship. We should shudder with great horror over this sin. He says that the Israelites have "exchanged their Glory for worthless idols." (Jeremiah 2:11).

By the way, I love how honest the Word of God is. I guess that's why we call it *truth*. He can call it what it is, and just proclaim the brokenness of their sin. It is a much simpler, honest way of living. It is simply what it is.

What happens when you worship idols? Jeremiah tells us that the Lord said that it will cause us to stumble (Jeremiah 18:15). When we put something other than the Lord on a pedestal, it becomes a god.

This eventually leads us to forget the one true God who reigns over heaven and earth.

For the Israelites, they had *gods* they would worship. We read about Baal who was thought to be translated into any number of generic gods. The literal meaning is lord or master. Jeremiah explains how determined the Israelite's were in worshipping their gods.

In Chapter 44, Jeremiah gives us an example of what these people were doing. There was a goddess of sexual love and fertility, the "Queen of Heaven." As Jeremiah is warning these people of the doom that they will bring on themselves, they answer:

> *"We will not listen to the message you have spoken to us in the name of the Lord! We will certainly do everything we said we would: We will burn incense to the Queen of Heaven"*
> *Jeremiah 44:16-17*

I read this and think, *how stubborn and arrogant are these people*, and then I am quietly and gently reminded of the gods that I struggle with.

My gods aren't called anything like queens, gods, or goddesses. No, those would be way too easy to identify. My gods are called perfectionism, money, performance, and family. All these are good things that God created that have slipped from being a *thing* to becoming something more important than God.

I realized that family was an idol for me after my accident when I waited for them to rescue me. They never rescued me because only God could do that. I realized that the god of perfectionism was genuinely devastated by my failure, and I only received condemnation when I looked to it. There was nothing either pretty or perfect about what I was going through. I was just trying to breath. I no longer cared about my hair color, keeping up with the latest trends or appearing put together. I just wanted to breathe.

I tried to fill my time with other activities. I used money as a source of finding fulfillment through shopping, and do extravagant things to only be left emptier than before. Anything other than God just left me more broken than before.

God created everything in the heavens and earth. We see something pure and wonderful that God gave us, and then we take it a step farther and attempt to use it to fill our empty hearts. In the same way, God created a way for the Israelites to make atonement for their sins through the sacrifices and offerings given to God on the altar. The Israelites however, took it one step further and began worshipping in ways that God never intended to false gods. Jeremiah tells us that there wasn't just occasional idol worship, but that it was common.

> *"You have as many gods as you have towns, O Judah; and the altars you have set up to burn incense to that shameful god Baal are as many as the streets of Jerusalem." Jeremiah 11:13*

The altar, a sacred place of offering their hearts to the one true God, became less important as they started doing whatever they wanted with it. A holy, significant and distinctive place where they connected to God in the beautiful exchange was left destitute and deserted. The people were fooled by their hearts into searching for something else that could fill the hole in their heart perhaps a little faster. These idols are all empty promises.

When disaster struck, these gods were silent.

How does God react? We see that His love cannot be shared with other gods. He is a jealous God because He wants you and me more than anything. When He watches as we suffer, He is the Father waiting with open arms to catch us. Yet so often we seek refuge in something tangible. It seems more reasonable to fill the emptiness with *things* or money instead of the quiet refuge that God brings through His peace.

Jeremiah tells us exactly how God felt about the Israelites as they offered their lives to other gods:

> *"The Lord Almighty, who planted you, has decreed disaster for you, because the house of Israel and the house of Judah have done evil*

and provoked me to anger by burning incense to Baal." Jeremiah 11:17

Can a god that doesn't mind sharing us truly love us? Our God won't share us and can fill all our needs. He can take care of fertility, the harvest, guidance, love and every other need we may have.

We are fooled into thinking that putting money first isn't necessarily a sinful thing. The Israelites were fooled into the same thinking. Remember, they were just a segment of the human population. It could have been you or me. Their idol worship led them to engage in one of the most detestable acts. Again, it's the **BEWARE** sign we are given as a warning.

Idol worship begins with small acts of sacrifice and eventually will lead to giving everything. For the Israelites, this led eventually to sacrificing their own children to try and please the pagan gods. Worshiping false gods lead to giving more and more until they were cold and calloused enough to offer their own children as an offering. Nothing would ever be sufficient to please the false gods.

Jeremiah reminds them several times that God neither commanded nor had this in mind (Jeremiah 7:31, 19:5). They were willing to give the blood of the innocent to foreign gods who couldn't fulfill any promise.

What will our gods lead us to give? Maybe today it is something small, but beware of what will be required tomorrow as the empty promises continually want more and more.

A prime example is when we chase the promise of youth. Plastic surgery after plastic surgery is a desperate attempt to fix our problems, yet every time we fix our *biggest issue* another rises to become the newest obsession. At what point do you stop?

Descriptions of both the tabernacle and Solomon's temple are described for us in the Bible. It appears that they were built in a logical order. For both structures, we read that they built the surrounding walls, curtains for the tabernacle and beautiful cedar for Solomon's temple. Then they filled the structure with the furnishings. The altar was most likely built sometime after the structure. There was no importance in the order that it was to be built.

For the exiles returning from Babylon, we read that they came together and they built the altar *first*. There was no structure up yet, no foundation laid, no other furnishings, and they built the altar.

The exiles came back from seventy years of Babylonian captivity, and they were determined to do things right. Their hearts realized that it wasn't a beautiful structure that God wanted, but their hearts. He wanted them, and He wanted them to want Him.

The very first thing they did after building that altar was to make burnt offerings to the Lord in the morning and in the evening. This was a symbolic act that showed they were fully and completely surrendered to God. They would lead their prized bull or ram to the altar and offer it without holding back to say *we only want you*. Over the seventy years of captivity, they realized that all God wanted was their hearts. The truth was that the temple wasn't as important as their hearts.

God promised that as the exiles returned they would be different. They would have undivided hearts and new spirits. Their hearts that had initially been turned to stone by stubbornness and lies would be changed back to flesh. What was the result? They would willingly follow God, and a beautiful exchange would happen:

> *"They will be my people, and I will be their God" Ezekiel 11:20*

Humbleness to bow your head and acknowledge you aren't in control is what we must bring to the altar. The Israelites realized they were sinners and that they deserved to pay for their sins. The pathway of sin leads to death. We deserve to die for sins. For the Israelites, they would watch as the bull or ram was taken to the altar. The animal would probably be struggling. They would hear the struggling animal and see the gruesome blood that was shed and realize that *that bull, or that ram, died for me.* In witnessing such a sight, they would be reminded of the weight of their sin and that it wasn't free. A reminder every morning and every evening that they were sinners and that they were coming to God through their own accord.

In the same way, in our journey, we realize that we are sinners and have nothing to offer God that is significant enough to save us. It is by the Lamb of God that we are saved, through His blood God accepts us. How easy it is to forget?

During my recovery, I began to have some horrible dreams as Satan was trying to break me down. It was the sin that I was holding on to that allowed Satan into my life. I believed it was too ugly to release to God, a holy God. A close friend asked me if I thought the price that Christ paid on the cross was enough, and I replied "absolutely." She helped me realize that my defiant, cold, hard grasp on these sins claimed that *the cross was not enough*. When that sank in, I remember being horrified at the realization that I was indeed turning Jesus away. Jesus died on the cross and did it for those sins.

Right then and there, I handed it over to God, and a dark, dense cloud was lifted, and I was set free. Jesus can't pay for what we aren't willing to hand over. I know that if I had lived over 2,000 years ago, was a believer and follower of Christ, and witnessed as Christ was crucified on the cross, I would immediately hand over my sins. I can imagine standing at the cross and watching Him suffer. I believe that I would be so overwhelmed by His love that I wouldn't ever take it for granted.

We can't hide our sin from God. In a bizarre trade, He loves us so much that He wants to cancel it out. He proved His dedication when He sent His only son to die for us.

The question to ask is this; *"Do I agree to lift my heart up to Him?"* As the Israelites fled the Egyptian captivity, God asked them if they were willing to follow Him as he rescued, provided and led them to the Promised Land. They all replied with a *"we will."* Will you? Will you answer with an *"I will follow you, through this season of devastation?"* We have to realize that it is only our heart that God wants in this exchange.

Before any rebuilding can happen in our lives, we must bring our hearts to God as our offering. The blessing of living through tragedy is it quickly shines a light on where your heart actually lies. Three years ago, my dad was diagnosed with a brain tumor. It wasn't a cancerous type of tumor, but it was still frightening. He would have to have it removed, and so we waited three long months before he had it removed. The surgery was scheduled five days before Christmas. Watching him lying in the hospital bed, convinced he wouldn't live through the recovery made me dig deep. I had nothing at that moment other than to hand my heart over to God and ask for help. In my desperation, I was reminded that there was someone who already knew the plan. At that moment I had no choice but to believe that He was going to walk us through this fire. He would lead us one step at a time.

If you are lucky enough, you will be in a place of desperation one day that will leave you crying out for help, and we all know where our help comes from.

"I lift my eyes up to the hills- where does my help come from? My help comes from the Lord, the Maker of heaven and earth" Psalms 121:1-2

Acknowledging that I was so broken on the inside that I had nothing to give God was right where God needed me. He needed me there. In the same way, God needed the Babylonian captives there. Through my tears, He could finally be my God, and I could be His child.

The exiles did nothing else before building the altar. They needed God. In the same way, I realized that there was no other place to go for help, but to God. My friends and family had no answers. My money and possessions seemed insignificant. My perfectionism and performance record were destroyed in an instant. I had nothing but my heart, and to be completely honest, even my heart felt worthless in its broken and shattered state.

I was so haunted by the spiritual attacks that it required giving my heart to God morning, afternoon, night (and usually several times throughout the night). I learned that I didn't have to guess how much love God had for me. How can you deny the depth of love He has when we read that His Beloved Son was sent to die for me?

How could I give such a sweet gift back to Him? My heart was the only thing I could put on the altar. It was all I had. Amazingly, it was all that He wanted.

Helps-Word Studies translates that the altar is a "*meeting place between God and the true worshiper, where the Lord meets and communes with the sincere believer.*" An altar doesn't work if you aren't sincere. This is why Jesus told the crowd in the Sermon on the Mount that when they approached the altar and have issues with a brother, they are to leave their gift until they are reconciled with that brother. God wants your sincere heart.

What are you willing to give? Are you going to offer a piece or all of your heart? In Genesis,

Chapter 22, God told Abraham to take his only son, Isaac up to make a burnt offering (an offering showing your full commitment to God). We all know that the story ends with God giving Abraham a ram at the last minute. Because of Abraham's dedication to God, he is told;

> *"Because you have done this and have not withheld your son, your only son, I will surely bless you and make your descendants as numerous as the stars in the sky and as the sand on the seashore." Genesis 22:16-17*

Isn't it incredible that God doesn't ask us to give back the same type of gift that He has given to us? While he was testing Abraham, His love would never demand the same gift that He so willingly gave to us.

The blessing of going through hard times is it drives you to a place where your heart is available to completely give to God. He, in turn, is able to bless you abundantly through that. Just as the Babylonian exiles realized the priority through their tragedy, we do as well.

God instructed the Israelites in Exodus to offer God the fat from the animals. In those days, the fat was considered to be the *prime rib* of our day. It was the best cut of meat. The fat that was burned as the Israelite offering to God would give off a sweet smell that would rise to God in heaven and was a "pleasing aroma" (Leviticus 3:16). I wonder how sweet the aroma is when we offer our hearts to Him and say *"this is all I have and it is all for You God, may it be a pleasing aroma to you?"*

It was this level of dedication through Jesus' love for us that He was willing to give His life as a fragrant offering to God (Ephesians 5:2). The blessing, for those of us who have confronted our greatest nightmare will realize, is that the only hope we have is God, and because of that it will make our dedication deeper and stronger if we will offer our hearts to Him.

Unfortunately, some of us will become a land of jackals through our suffering. We will become a desolate place that is dark and dry. Others of us will turn away the jackals at the altar and let God lead us through the recovery process. This process will feel like an exile and wilderness at times. We will follow God step by step as the returning exiles did. Just as they began to rebuild their temple, we too will find the tools to rebuild.

Meeting God at our altar, tells Him that even though are life is in shambles; He still reigns!

CHAPTER SEVEN

LAYING THE FOUNDATION

Center Everything Around the Altar

I'm out of control. There's good news, though. I'm not the only one. You are out of control as well. No matter how hard you are fighting for control, you still have none. You can't control what tomorrow holds. Some of us can walk through life pretending that we have complete control of our lives, but still this lingering truth remains.

This was perhaps the hardest part of the healing process from the car accident. I set out on that May 9th with high expectations. I was hesitant to leave my newborn but found an ounce of courage to conquer my goals that day. How is it that a person can be doing everything in the best way they know, following all the rules, and trying their best and still find themselves in the midst of a nightmare?

After the accident, I stared down fate. The future that is entirely unknown to me and will continue to be out of my hands no matter how noble, courageous, brave or loving a person I am. We have no control of our lives.

The fact remains that I can leave my house tomorrow morning doing everything right and I can face my biggest nightmare. Do you realize that you take the same chance? If we were to look into a crystal ball and watch as our lives played out, would we have the courage to face tomorrow?

Even the Word of God tells us not to worry about tomorrow, most likely for that exact reason. I'm not convinced I would have the courage if I knew how my story played out. I am even more convinced that I would never let go of those that mean the most of me if I knew how their story played out.

What we do have control over is the foundation that we lay in our life. This foundation is what dictates how we handle our tomorrows. How we prepare and prioritize will significantly influence not only how we handle struggle, but also our strength to be the light of the world. The work that we do today matters for tomorrow.

The exiles returned to their desolate home after seventy years of captivity. They build the altar, and then we are told that they begin to lay the foundation. For the temple, the foundation is the underlying structure that holds everything else up.

In our lives, the foundation is the structure that we build our life on. Our foundation is centered on our hearts, just as the exiles built their foundation around the altar for God.

Just as some foundations are terrible and crack and fall away, others can stand for hundreds and hundreds of years. A few years ago we bought a home built in the 1950's. It's a small house nestled in an older neighborhood. There's a Snyders neighborhood grocery store with a small ice cream bar inside. You can almost just see a different time in American culture with kids playing on the street and getting their nickle to go down and get ice cream after their family dinner.

Buying a house from this date can be a bit intimidating as you never know what issues will arise. As we walked behind the inspector looking over the foundation wondering what major deal breaking flaw he would find, we were shocked to hear his verdict. He said, "This was a well-built home, with a good foundation." His evaluation of the foundation was such a relief and honestly was a make it or break it moment for us. Now don't misunderstand me here, there were flaws from the years that the house has stood, but the foundation was good. Everything else can be fixed or appreciated for its character, but the foundation mattered.

In the midst of tragedy, it will feel like you have a building inspector in your soul to inspect your foundation. Some of us will watch as the whole foundation crumbles away, while some of us are abundantly blessed by the help, strength, and love our foundation brings.

In the midst of my tragedy, I found myself with my daughter and my husband in the middle of a big city with very little. What I didn't have didn't seem to matter as much as what I did have. I had a few good friends that sat beside me. I had a reason to keep breathing when I looked at my baby girl. I had a man that made me feel safe and secure in the middle of the night after I had a nightmare. I had a church that encouraged me. I had a small group that I could be completely honest with. My foundation may not have looked like a lot, but what I had was what got me through. One common saying that is true during tragedy is, *you find out who your real friends are.* The priorities, friends, church, education, etc. will determine how prepared you are to deal with a tragedy.

In the New Testament, the apostle Paul warns us about the type of foundation we lay. He tells us that we can build whatever we want on our foundations (gold, silver, stone, wood, hay or straw), but that eventually the fire will come through and test the quality of our work. He was speaking of our life in general as we near our final judgment. The foundations that survive will receive the reward while those that are burned will be lost. (1 Corinthians 3:10-15)

So, we do get control over something. This is great news for people such as me who love to feel in control. We get to control how we build our foundations.

A sturdy foundation has got to be ultimately built upon the cornerstone of Jesus Christ, though. When the exiles built the temple, we see the word of the Lord came through the prophet Haggai. Through those words, we witness the frustration that God had with the exiles. I often wonder if these are the same frustrations He has with most of us as well.

> *"This is what the Lord Almighty says; "Give careful thought to your ways. Go up into the mountains and bring down timber and build the house of God, so that I may take pleasure in it, and be honored," says the Lord." Haggai 1:7-8*

It is to Gods glory that we produce much. He takes pleasure in our foundations. As He inspects our foundations, I can only imagine the joy when they stand through the fire. I can't even imagine the honor that we bring to Him when we have a well laid foundation.

Through my journey there were many ways, my foundation went up in flames. My foundation was based on an idea of who God was and not the truth. I felt like such a disappointment to Him in so many ways before my accident. I loved Him, though, and that love kept my foundation from turning into coals. I noticed that my foundation became stronger each day that I leaned on Him. When my heart was centered on my pride and earthly promises my foundation was made of sinking sand. I would lose my strength and the fulfilling love that He so desperately wanted to send straight to my hungry heart. When I was humble and able to lean on Him and not my own understanding all the Glory would go to Him. It was beyond my strength. Everyone around me knew it as well.

I found that when I was asked about the situation, I had a huge choice to make. I could either be honest which made me vulnerable, or I could be a stone and tell everyone I was fine. Shutting the walls of brokenness down would only leave me empty.

Opening my heart and letting the vulnerability sweep through always lead to the pathway of love. This love would flow from others, and I would feel the love of God surround me. My foundation would always strengthen, and I could physically feel it. Vulnerability led to the people in my life helping me carry the weight of the pain I had on my shoulders.

Parts of my foundation that were merely scrapped materials quickly burned away. I could almost see them disappear as they meant nothing in the toughest moments. Fun things that I had usually cared so much about like drinking in bars, unhealthy relationships, money, and cars all quickly disappeared in flames. The weight of the pain was overbearing to these building materials. You could almost see the snapping joints that couldn't withstand the trial.

If this seems a bit overwhelming, just remember scripture leads us through building our foundation. Foundations will be tested through fire and will certainly burn up if not properly built. Our God who is forever merciful and loving will never require us to build our foundation alone. My story is full of blessings that gave me a helping hand during the building process. Most importantly, though, God is on our side as we lay the precious materials and make that foundation built on Him. He takes great and sweet pleasure in watching our foundations as they withstand all that the enemy throws at them.

There are a couple of foundational, unceasing truths that you have to allow your heart to accept, though.

Who God Is and Why He Accepts You

A common saying in our house, especially with the kids is that *knowledge is power*. I am thoroughly convinced of that truth.

I grew up by one of the largest manmade lakes in the world located in Arizona and Utah, called Lake Powell. Known for its crystal clear, warm water and fantastic fishing I took its beauty for granted. It wasn't until after I left home that I realized how amazing it was to spend my summers on a lake that people travel all over the world to visit.

It is the Colorado River that is held by Glen Canyon Dam that creates this amazing lake. The Dam is a massive 710 feet high. Standing on the dam and seeing a lake on one side and looking off the other side to the Colorado River you grasp how much water that concrete is holding back. We would often kayak that Colorado River in the summer and would start at the Dam and float down the river. It is a frightening experience. You have to trust that the dam is going to hold that water. At first glance, trust would be impossible. How can concrete stop a force of nature such as that lake coming through? As you learn more about the structure, though, your trust begins to grow. You learn that the damn is much thicker than it looks. It's not one foot thick, or ten feet thick or even 50 feet thick. It is an amazing 300 feet thick.

When you begin to trust the structure, then you learn the other functions of the dam. It was built to also provide hydroelectricity. There is a beautiful design that you would totally miss if you didn't learn more about it.

As I began the rebuilding process and building a stronger foundation in my life, I realized that I didn't trust God. Now I realize that I just didn't understand the true character of God.

I was baptized at nine and attended church my whole life, but for some reason, I believed that God was a God who would turn His back on His people. I knew He sent His son, but I truly believed that He was unforgiving of our sins. I believed that He expected perfection from those who followed Him. I believed that He would look at us in disgust when we made a mistake. It makes sense then that I didn't want to burden Him with my sinfulness.

Writing those words breaks my heart today. How horrifying it is to write those words of our God. However, I realize that my foundation got rocked so hard because I didn't understand our amazing, merciful, and gracious God. I didn't understand my God that I was forcing myself to put my trust and faith in.

One thing I am fascinated by the Old Testament is you get to see so much of God's own words. We have an opportunity to learn so much about God in the Old Testament. We can put everything we have ever heard about God on the back burner and see firsthand how He talks to the people in the Old Testament and His great love for His people. If I had any confidence to build a foundation it came through truly knowing God more deeply. The more I learned, the more I built. I was laying the concrete without realizing it every time I discovered a new truth about God.

When faced with a tragedy or even just a season of trials we have to convince our mind that God isn't off in some distant area. God hasn't overlooked us. He is certainly not punishing us like an angry parent. He's not overwhelmed by the problems of the world. His grasp on reality isn't overwhelming to Him as it is to us. He has control. What I found is that my tragedy was a sweet calling to run to His arms.

The problem is that understanding and comprehending where God is *now* is hard to fully comprehend. We teach our kids that He sits up in the clouds, and then our children (us) grow up thinking that maybe God was too high up to see what happened to us on our bad days. We believe that God is out of touch and that is the lie Satan would love for us to believe. Our foundation immediately becomes stronger when we accept that God is here right now. God is transcendent. Therefore, He is here with me as I write this, and He is there with you as you read this. He is nearby, and faraway. He is hiding in your secret place with you, as well as with me. He loves each and every individual on the other side of the world just the same as His deep love touches my heart. Sometimes, seeking wisdom means admitting that we may not fully understand some things.

It is true that He fills the heavens. Whether that means *in the clouds* or not, I'm not sure. However, He also fills the earth, and He has declared to us that it is true (Jeremiah 23:23-34). I love that God is described to be near, which is the Hebrew word of *Qarob*, meaning at hand. Do you believe that *God is at hand*? When I struggle with feeling alone, I look at my hand and believe that God is right there.

If God is right here (there), then we ask what we think he does when you are broken. Does He turn a blind eye to our pathetic mess? No. His eyes are on you. His ears are on you. His full attention is on you. Can you believe that He is all yours? When you cry out, He hears. When your heart is broken, He is close. When your spirit it crushed, He is there wanting to save you. This is our God. Our foundation is solid when it's built upon having a God who is near. He is near all the time and all attentive to our pleas and cries. (Psalms 34:15-18)

Commonly, we ask, *if there is a God then why does He allow this*?

I recently heard a story about a woman who believed in God, until her husband was diagnosed with cancer. The husband couldn't handle the diagnosis, so he killed himself. She decided that if there were a God, He wouldn't have allowed this to happen. I asked the same question after my accident, *"God if you are really there, why would you allow this to happen?"* Perhaps you have asked the same question of God.

After reading through the Bible in search of that answer, I realized that it's because of love. How can I be the light of the world if I never have anything bad happen? If I lived a perfect life, how could I relate to those going through a nightmare? Would they even care what I had to say if I couldn't relate to their grief? Would we have most people spending eternity in Hell because God cared more about making my life comfortable? How can God truly love all of us if He doesn't send anyone to help this dying world? And if He doesn't break my heart for this world, how can He truly love yours?

I also realized that God never promised me a perfect life while I walk this earth. In fact, he says:

"A righteous man may have many troubles, but the Lord delivers him from them all" Psalms 34:19

As we read through the Israelites story, they were asking the same questions. They were filled with the same doubt that we struggle with. We witness in their story that they continually worshipped idols. They got sent into captivity after being warned time after time to turn from these sinful and selfish ways. After getting sent into exile, they have the audacity to doubt God. What would have happened if God just lets them continue to worship idols? Surely, we wouldn't want to see the destruction they would find without God.

What I have come to realize about God and the Israelites is this; could a God that didn't fight for His children even love them? If I can put it in terms we understand today it would sound like a soap opera, but I'll go there anyways. If a woman is cheating on her husband and her husband just ignores it, did he ever truly love her, to begin with? If he never stopped to fight for her or to work things out, was his heart even in the relationship? Surely not.

In Jeremiah, it says that God allows the Israelites into captivity to teach the Israelites. He will teach them of His power and His might so that they may be blessed by fully knowing who He is (Jeremiah 16:21). That puts a different spin on the situation.

After going through my car accident, all the false things I believed about God were proved false. They were burned up. I had never felt closer to God as in those moments. The less I thought I knew about God, the more I felt His loving embrace. As I looked upward and cried out, I learned that He was near me. I felt the love He had for me. In those moments, He was teaching me who He was. I can honestly say that I have never been so blessed to see Him so clearly.

A foundation can only be as strong as we can acknowledge Gods love is for us. We can absentmindedly claim that God loves us and that He sent His son for our sins. But recognizing the whole story and accepting His abundant love changes everything.

I find it incredible that He sent His son to die for us after a history of His people turning to other gods, over and over again. They continually doubted God. They questioned who He is, what He has done and so He did something that would save us. He sent His son to die. The old covenant was destroyed, and through Christ, we are able to fully know who God is.

Do you know what the new covenant guaranteed to each of us? This is what you were given when you placed your trust in the blood of Jesus that was shed:

> *"I will put my laws in their minds and write them on their hearts. I will be their God, and they will be my people. No longer will a man teach his neighbor, or a man his brother, saying, "Know the Lord," because they will all know me, for the least of them to the greatest. For I will forgive their wickedness and will remember their sins no more" Jeremiah 31:31-34*

This is who our God is. This is what our foundation must be. It doesn't matter what you are going through right now. You can be on top of the world or beg for leftovers behind a restaurant, and we all have the same opportunity to know God the Father. He sits at hand.

Make it Sturdy

This morning on the news I witnessed another devastating earth quake in Italy. Pictures of piles of wreckage lined the streets. So many buildings were so damaged they appeared to be more of a pile of rocks instead of beautiful homes that they have been for hundreds of years. I noticed something behind these piles of rubble. As they continued to pull bodies out, I noticed the buildings that still stood. One building you could see was at least 3-4 stories higher than the rest with what appeared to be a bell at the top. My first thought was, how in the world did that structure stand when everything else around it is a mess? I imagine that the day before the earth quake no one truly knew which ones would stand and which would fall. They never knew the potential of the buildings until they were tested.

I believe we are the same. We don't realize our full potential. We fail to take the time and invest in ourselves, in building a strong foundation because we don't value ourselves enough. We don't realize how resilient and strong God has created us to be. We instead chase worldly desires to keep ourselves preoccupied. We forget each day we are warned to have strong foundations.

We aren't called to build foundations that measure up to the world's standards. Those are the foundations that look good. They are attractive in sight. They hold immediate promises that are never delivered. When tested, they burn up. We are called to live by the laws of God. We are called to put all our eggs in His basket, and to follow Him and to rest at the foot of the cross. No matter the cost.

Jeremiah shares with us his secret to being a living stone. Remember Jeremiah was a man that didn't conform to the world. His frustration is likely the same feeling you have as you try so hard to do the right things while everyone else cuts corners. You aren't alone, though. Jeremiah reminds us that the Word of God is more than just words, but:

> *"His word is in my heart like a fire, a fire shut up in my bones. I am weary of holding it in; indeed, I cannot" Jeremiah 20:9*

If there was any question how Jeremiah went against the culture to speak truth, I believe we just witnessed his secret. This is strength. This same strength is available to anyone who wants it. Jeremiah endures through life because he witnesses that God is with him like a "mighty warrior" (Jeremiah 20:11).

As a coach tells their athlete a step by step to winning the game, I believe the Holy Spirit whispers to us how to build our foundation. We are called to have strong foundations. These foundations aren't guided by humans, but by God. The foundations are so strong that we can't overlook injustices when called by God to be strong. As we transform into living stones and continually begin looking more and more like Jesus, we can't keep the words of God out of our mouth. When the words are from God, the strength from God and the laws of God; our life can't help but bring Him glory. In that, He finds great pleasure I'm sure.

Hold Nothing Back

We live in a society that tries to turn us into hoarders. We stock pile money, clothes, food, and the like. We save our money in hopes of having a great retirement when none of us are even guaranteed a retirement. We stock up supplies in hopes of one day doing something. We keep an old pair of skis in hopes of eventually learning how to water ski. Take a walk through someone's house and ask about random items and you'll find out how we all struggle in one way or another when none of us are guaranteed anything in the future. We hang onto our own plan and agenda, often unknowingly because our faith in God's plan isn't where it needs to be. This type of mentality will leave you broken in the midst of a tragedy. The wakeup call will come when you realize your foundation was set on your own plans and is completely irrelevant.

When Solomon set out to build the first temple, we are told that he spared no expense to build a place where God could alone be worshiped in a centralized place of worship. Although, we see Solomon wasn't perfect as he poured just as much money and in fact, more time into his own palace, he didn't spare a dime on the Temple. He was rewarded for trying to have the right idea, even though it became clouded with a little bit of greed.

Our foundations are being built correctly when we are focused on God, and everything else in our world conforms to that. We hold nothing back to serving God. I'm not talking about giving every penny you have away. I think its Satan scheme to make us feel inadequate with what we give. I'm talking about not holding any part of your HEART back. Your foundation is strong with each piece of your heart that you hand over to God.

As I read about the exiles building their foundation of the temple, it so much reminds me of my own struggle. The building of the foundation was described in Ezra 3:7-11. The initial step for the people was to give money to the people of surrounding areas to obtain the cedar logs needed to build the temple. They knew they wouldn't be able to build the temple by themselves. They could have tried, but they realized the importance and the cost their pride would cost them. How often we attempt to do the same thing in our own lives. We struggle until we are about to break before we ask for help. God has blessed us by giving us a family bigger than just the people from the same family lineage. Brothers and sisters in Christ are pulled together in the same spirit to wade through the troubles of this world. A properly built foundation will require some help.

Not only are we going to need some help, but we will need some honesty. As the Israelites were building the temple, they appointed specific people to supervise the process. To be designated to this supervisory role there were requirements. Mainly the person would have been a Levite, 20 years or older. I could speculate here on these qualifications, but the more important piece for us that they didn't trust just anyone.

As you are deliberate about your foundation, be specific who you will let supervise. Those people will tell you when priorities seem skewed. They will have the courage to tell you when you are out of line, or when your sinful nature is catching up with you. A word of caution - you can only fully rely on others who lean on God for their own understanding to help guide you. Be deliberate. You deserve a well-qualified friend who can help guide you on your journey.

As I struggled to wade through my own grief after my accident, I had a dear mentor that drove a knife straight into the poison that continually chipped away at my foundation. She pointed out my codependency that was causing so much grief in my life. This codependency affected relationships in my life negatively in so many different facets. As she identified it, I knew she wanted my foundation to be firm and so out of love she pointed it out. I appreciate her wise supervision as I was laying my foundation.

This can be a very humbling experience. But, building a foundation alone can feel like baking a cake without the recipe. You can do it over and over again to only pull a pancake out of the oven, or you can lean on the recipe and do it right the first (second or third) time. Without the recipe, how many times would you try and bake a cake before you just gave up? After all, it would be much easier to buy a beautiful one at the grocery store.

After the Israelites completed the painful process of laying the foundation, came the exciting part of the journey. I can almost imagine them standing around the foundation with tears in their eyes as they realize that the next step is to make this a reality. They could start dreaming on what is to be built. After all the hard work and dedication to getting the foundation right, they do something that must be music to God's ears. They celebrate.

> *"With praise and thanksgiving they sang to the Lord: He is good; his love to Israel endures forever. And all the people gave a great shout of praise to the Lord because the foundation of the house of the Lord was laid."*
> *Ezra 3:11*

What a victory! The people look out amongst this newly built foundation and recognize the work that God has done.

In this same way, we look at our transforming life. We find it filled with an unimaginable peace and recognize that this is the work that God has done. You will recognize this point when your foundation is laid correctly by the overwhelming harmony of the relationship with God you have and how that has affected everything else in your life. You know it's time to celebrate with praise and thanksgiving.

As a home owner, my favorite shows to watch are the home renovation shows on HGTV. I particularly enjoy the shows that show people buying up old homes and renovating them. It is always devastating news when the home owner discovers a bad foundation. When the foundation is bad everything else stops. Renovating the foundation isn't exciting. You don't see the foundation, there is nothing to spice it up to make it look shiny or attractive, but it is the most important aspect of a home. With a bad foundation, nothing else matters. Wallpaper, paint, tile, decorations all become irrelevant until that foundation is fixed.

Your life and mine are the same. Until the foundation is laid correctly, our world will resemble the shambles that we feel on the inside. There will be a great victory for the work that is put into it. The process of laying a foundation in our life can be very painful. The process of rejecting sin and accept God's ways over our own isn't an easy journey.

Tragedy brings us to a place that we are so broken that our only option is to build the foundation right. The structure we have built on a bad foundation falls away, and we start to build again. I pray we build with the right materials. I believe that you start to breathe when you build it on the Cornerstone.

And then the celebration is probably marked by the transformation from broken to the first smile that begins to reemerge on your face.

CHAPTER EIGHT

FINDING OUR STRENGTH

Compelled by the Spirit

It's that moment in your life when you just don't know how to take the next step. For me, it was getting in my husband's truck to go home from the accident sight. It was the first time getting behind the steering wheel. It was waking up from a nightmare of the replay of the entire accident. It was seeing a movie that had a dead body and recognizing the eyes from the man I hit. It was driving by the accident scene and seeing the cross that marked a life that was lost there. It was the daily reminder of all the unanswered questions that I had.

For others, it's laying down the pen from signing the divorce papers. It's the next breath after hearing a loved one has passed away. It's walking out of the funeral home after picking the coffin for a child. These next steps are the ones that are impossible. The strength these steps take is impossible to measure. It's these steps that no one can understand but those of us that walk them. I do believe that we have all walked these steps before though. Every single one of them, unique.

If you have walked these steps before, I think we find a sense of peace that we aren't alone. For the exiles that had returned this moment is documented for us all to walk through with them. There was a moment after the foundation is laid that they questioned if they would be able to go on. As many of the people were celebrating the laying of the foundation, the writer of Ezra explains of an opposing emotion as well:

> *"But many of the older priests and Levites and family heads, who had seen the former temple, wept aloud when they saw the foundation of this temple being laid, while many others shouted for joy. No one could distinguish the*

sound of the shouts of joy from the sound of weeping because the people made so much noise. And the sound was heard from far away"
Ezra 3:12-13

Those people who saw the beautiful temple of Solomon, richly adorned with precious metals and decorations knew that the supplies the exiles had to rebuild could never compare. As they watched the rebuilding, I imagine that they feared it could never be the same. The people celebrating were probably the ones that never experienced the temple before. They never knew of the beauty that would never be again.

In our own life, that moment of watching the temple walls fall down our initial thought is that we will never be the same. This is true. What we remember being will change as we grow through the experience. The things that we think are important, such as our innocence will be lost as our eyes are painfully opened. The unknown of what will take place is scary. We will often believe that there is no way something beautiful will come out of this mess. I can remember wondering if it was possible to ever be happy again. I knew that the old me was gone, forever changed and that is perhaps the scariest realization to accept. We dread change, especially when there is so much unknown involved and there's no going back.

This doubt did not only come from my own heart. I could see the doubt on the faces around me. *"Will she ever be the same?"*, *"What will become of her?"*, and *"Such a pity..."*. Now, I must admit that how valid this thought is I'm not sure, but I felt like I could read it on faces around me. In the midst of the battle, I felt like people had already thrown in the towel to mourn the loss of my soul.

What is it that will give us the strength to take the next step into the unknown? People will say there is no easy answer to that question, but I disagree. The answer is a lot easier than we generally think.

Two men are listed by name that were instrumental during this process of the Israelites trying to find their strength. The prophets Haggai and Zechariah prophesied to the people. The prophet Haggai encouraged the people to have spiritual vitality and reminded the people of the blessing that was to follow. Zechariah, on the other hand, was a motivator. He gave them a vision that was beyond the painful toil of building the temple.

Zechariah's word of motivation for Zerubbabel who was the leader of the disheartened Jews was a reminder of where the strength will come from to finish building.

"Not by might nor by power, but by my spirit, says the Lord Almighty" Zechariah 4:6

There is no secret to being strong. There is no amount of earthly power, or determination, or stubbornness that we can find to give us the strength to get through this life. The answer to finding strength is through the Spirit. Period. The Holy Spirit is our Great Comforter, our Helper sent straight from the Father (John 15:26). Zerubbabel may have been the greatest leader of all times, but there is nothing he could do on his own that would calm the fears of the people who had been through such a horrific time.

Haggai (the encourager) heard from God on the same subject, and God wanted Haggai to reassure Zerubbabel and all the people of where to find their strength:

> *"Who of you is left who saw this house in its former glory? How does it look to you now? Does it not seem to you like nothing? But now be strong, O Zerubbabel, declares the Lord. Be strong, O Joshua son of Jehozadak, the high priest. Be strong, all you people of the land, declares the Lord, and work. For I am with you, declares the Lord Almighty. This is what I covenanted with you when you came out of Egypt. And my Spirit remains among you. Do not fear." Haggai 2:3-5*

Do you remember what you were before? Do you think you are nothing now? Those words just almost bring me to my knees. I remember all too well. If you fall apart reading those words, you know what I mean. A parent that has lost a child will understand this difference. A person who just went through a divorce, an abused person, a bankrupt person, a newly diagnosed cancer patient and the list goes on and on. We remember what once was. We remember…

Be strong because His Spirit is with you. Cast all your worries upon Him and take one step at a time. Worry less about what your life will become and more of where God needs you right at that moment. In those moments of complete fear, we must remind ourselves of the strength of the Spirit that is willing to carry us through if we allow. It is scary, but be strong. Do not fear. Reach out to the Great Comforter who is at hand.

For me, I clung to any reminder to trust God. To find trust that He had me, my tomorrow and my far away future I quoted a verse over and over. In fact, this verse brought me such peace that I had it painted onto our bedroom wall so that I would be reminded of it as I went to sleep. As I was awakened from nightmares and as I arose fearful in the morning I would read these words. Psalms 46:10:

"Be still and know that I am God."

An easy and simple verse, but that verse carried me through my most fearful times. I would repeat it over and over and allow myself to rely on the strength of the Spirit as I calmed my fears down. It is that moment when no one in your life can give you the strength you need to get through, but you say a verse of eight words and you feel like you can carry on, that you are certain of the truth of who God is. If that seems unbelievable, I challenge you to try it.

The other reminder that we see through the words of Haggai and Zechariah is that God understands our thoughts. The psalmist also understood what it was like to have anxious thoughts and tells us that it is God's comfort that overcomes these emotions (Psalms 94:19 and Psalms 139:23).

I had moments when memories of the accident would come flooding into my mind. To translate that image to anyone around me would have been cruel to them and cruel to me, but yet I never had to tell God. He always knew them. He saw them and understood the reason for my anxiousness.

We were never expected to have every emotion under control. We aren't God. We were not created to understand and control everything. What we do with those thoughts is what we have control over. God understood the fear that the Jewish people had. He understood their thoughts more than they even did. He understood why it was hard for them to rebuild a temple. It is pure love that He speaks to Haggai and Zechariah to reassure Zerubbabel and the people to rely on Him for strength.

Unfortunately, the remembrance of what the temple was not the hardest part for the Jews. They encountered considerable opposition of the rebuilding process. The opposition to the rebuilding stalled the process for 16 whole years. The process of reconstruction isn't in a specific time frame for us either. We are never promised a smooth ride ahead either. For me, just as I was coming around to finding my foundation (which was leading to happiness), we got the knock on the door. I was getting sued.

It was a quiet evening about six months after the accident. We were at our house as we were getting ready for the pizza to be delivered. I was sitting on the couch with my baby girl, and then the doorbell rang. Expecting it to be the pizza I didn't hesitate. It was the tone of my husband's voice that alerted me. As I walked toward to the door, I knew what was happening I just couldn't fully comprehend what it meant. My panic jumped out of the roof at that moment not knowing how I was going to handle this. At that moment, the overbearing weight of the accident came flooding back in. I just wanted this nightmare to be over. I was then reminded to *be still*. We handled it one day at a time, one question at a time. We did it together and leaned on the Great Comforter.

This process took months after we found out we were being sued by the family. For weeks, I had been hurt and angry, then angry then hurt. It was quite the rollercoaster of emotions. On one fateful day, after I had been drug through a terrible deposition a trusted friend encouraged me to forgive the family. It was a leap of faith. It basically required handing over my anxious thoughts to God as I asked for true forgiveness. As I relied on the spirit, my level of strength multiplied. Not only did I gain divine strength, but my world became a little brighter. It was as if a cloud finally passed from blocking the sun. I remember saying, *"The sun is shining again."*

On my way home, I stopped to get the mail and received a letter from our insurance company explaining the family had dropped the amount of the lawsuit so low that it was cheaper to pay them off than to continue to fight the case. A day earlier, it would have been traumatizing to know that the family would make a financial gain from this tragedy, but on that day all I received was peace. It was peace that the lawsuit was over. It was peace that I could rely on God to handle the justice or injustices. I could rest in the fact that I didn't fully understand the situation. On that day, my shackles and chains were loosened, and I was set free. I prayed that the family could find some peace as well and that the money could help them in some way.

The day that the Jews received their freedom was their fateful day after 16 long years of inactivity. It was their fear that stopped the progress, and relying on the Spirit is what pushed them through to finish it.

When they began rebuilding, the Word says that it was the "*eye of their God*" that protected them from finishing. They were building the walls of the temple with diligence and making rapid work of it, but when asked who it was that gave them their authority they were able to answer:

> "*We are the servants of the God of heaven and earth, and we are rebuilding the temple that was built many years ago, one that a great king of Israel built and finished*" Ezra 5:11

Finding our strength today, amongst people and darkness of this world, will require this same dedication. We are servants of the God of heaven and earth, and we are rebuilding the temple that was built many years ago, one that a great King of Israel built and finished. That temple is us. It was built many years ago by Jesus, the great King who died for us and gave us a new covenant that empowered each of us that believe in the Spirit. It was finished when He breathed

His last breath, hanging on that cross. This is who we are, and this is what we are doing.

Where does our strength come from? (Get ready because the simple answer should fill us with so much thankfulness for this precious gift) It comes from our God that views us as His precious, dearly loved temples. Keep building, my friend, as the precious eye of our God is with you.

CHAPTER NINE

BETTER THAN BEFORE

The Beauty That Comes from Disaster

Stone by stone, brick by brick the temple was built. It was built, indeed. There must have been a moment of silence as the people turned to take the first glance at their temple. With bruised bodies, calloused hands and weary souls they take the first look at what their years of toil resulted in.

The completed temple was built, and it was built according to God's commands. It took 22 years to build, and within those years the people encountered many opposition and trials. When they looked at the finished temple, they had to realize that they did it because of their perseverance. Did they remember all the moments of doubt or the back-breaking work each day required?

What else would they do after the moment of taking it all in? Of course, they had to do what we should all do after accomplishing something great. We are told they celebrated the dedication of their temple. Can you just imagine the great joy they felt? There must have been a sense of relief that they were obedient and it was worth every second.

Was the temple that they finished pleasing enough for them? Or were they still comparing the temple to the grandiosity of the temple that Solomon built? They must have been making comparisons wondering if what they accomplished was enough for God. Were the building materials expensive enough to bring glory to God? Was the linen's beauty sufficient to give God the credit He deserves? How will this temple ever measure up to what God deserves when it could never compare to the one before?

Walking through recovery from any tragedy or hardship will leave us asking the same question. As God rescues us from our grief and gives us the strength to continue to live, and we recognize the blessings that He has given us, there is no way our *temples* could ever do Him justice. We try to hide the scars that are left behind in fear that it will bring discredit to our God that has worked miracles in our life. How could the rebuilding of our temples ever give the credit due to our God? We know what God has done so how can we ever reflect an ounce of His glory?

Zerubbabel, the leader during this time had to of been exhausted. He must have been wondering all these same questions. Did he do well enough? Did he paint the vision well enough for the people? Did he complete the task according to what he was told to do?

In a beautiful moment, the prophet Haggai receives encouraging words from the Lord to give to Zerubbabel. After the Prophet explains where the Jews will find the strength to continue building, He gives Zerubbabel hope in what the future will look like:

> *"I will shake all nations and the desired of all nations will come, and I will fill this house with glory, says the Lord Almighty. The silver is*

mine and the gold is mine, declares the Lord
Almighty. The glory of this present house will
be greater than the glory of the former house,
says the Lord Almighty. And in this place I will
grant peace, declares the Lord Almighty."
Haggai 2:7-9

As the Jews looked upon their finished temple, they had to believe that what God said was true. This was going to bring more glory than that of the majestic temple that Solomon built. When Solomon's temple was torn down, there was a divine plan in place. God knew what He was doing. The same hope of future glory applies to you and me. As our temples are torn down, and we begin rebuilding our life, God has a plan in place. Our life isn't just a series of coincidences, but that of a deliberately laid out plan that will make us into beautiful temples. These new temples will be filled with more glory than before. This will translate into a divine peace that radiates to those around us. People will look at your life and wonder how in the world you are still standing after going through something so hard. Then they will see *it*. They will see and recognize the divine strength within you.

Grasping for understanding is dangerous and all so tempting. Will we lean on our own understanding? Will we try and find answers to our questions? This path leads to roadblocks every time. When we lean not on our own understanding, but our faithfulness we will find this divine strength to get out of bed every morning. I can't explain how this works, but I experienced it every day.

Each morning when I didn't believe I could look in the mirror, God would prove to me that He can do great things with our *messes*, and He will give us enough to take the first steps. There are two separate passages in the New Testament that assure us of this truth.

The first is in Romans, chapter 5. First, we have to know the background information of these chapters before we can truly appreciate the meaning of the message. The book of Romans was written by the Apostle Paul, who was formerly known as Saul. Saul's first appearance in the Bible begins in Acts, chapter 9 when he giving his approval to the stoning of Stephen for being a follower of God. His divine intervention by God changed his heart, and he became the Apostle Paul. He writes the book of Romans from his first-hand experience with God's grace. In chapter 5 (verse 3-5), he speaks of the peace that the Jews were assured of through the prophet Haggai. This peace, Paul tells us is achieved through our faith in Jesus. He says this is the reason why we are to rejoice in our sufferings.

That is such a hard verse to understand if you are in the middle of the muck. What we understand though as we rebuild our temples is how painfully true it is. We rejoice because we realize that there has been a transformation that has taken place in our life that is unlike anything this world could teach us. Paul tells us that the process goes like this:

Suffering →Perseverance →Character →Hope

The other passage in the New Testament that assures us of this truth is in James, Chapter 1 (verse 2-4). Most believe that James is written by Jesus's brother. If that is the truth, then we know that James is a man that can relate to suffering. Have you lost a sibling? Or maybe you have lost a person so near and dear to you that it rips your heart in two. James can relate to that pain. During the time that the book of James was written (40-50 A.D.) was a horrible time to be a Christian. Anyone living during the period after the crucifixion understood what suffering and persecution meant, yet James tells us to consider it joy when we face trials. The process he describes goes like this:

Trials→Perseverance→Maturity→Complete

What results from trials, struggles, tragedies, hardships, and adversities can produce something so much greater in you than could have ever been imagined. In the midst of the battle, you will struggle to convince yourself of the truth, but if you allow God to lead you through your brokenness, you will stand back and be amazed at how He has changed you. The glory of your temple will be greater than ever before, even with the scars.

As I have struggled through the past nine years of understanding, I am constantly reminded of this truth as nowhere in the Bible does it ever tell us that we will achieve perfection through a life of ease. God's Word reassures us of the opposite. So often we want to believe the world because it just seems so much easier.

The word *perseverance* that both James and Paul use to explain how suffering and trials lead us to be better should help us understand why it can feel as though it is the harder road to take. When we choose to follow God, the path may seem more daunting, and that is because it requires us to stay in the moment and accept our circumstances. Helps-Word Commentary tells us that the word *perseverance* here means that *"God enables the believer to remain under the challenges that God allots in our life."* It also is translated into a *"patient enduring."* This term is quite a rare quality in those of us that roam this world. There is usually nothing patient or enduring that comes naturally but is a quality we must choose.

If you attempt to escape your circumstances, you will miss the opportunity of being blessed abundantly. All escaping will lead to is a life of denial. Eventually, you have to harden your heart to a level that exceeds the calling of God in your life. You must make a choice to *remain under* the challenges that you are facing. There will be two separate pathways set before you. Jeremiah warned that the Israelites had the same decision to make. They would have to decide whether they would follow God, even though it meant being taken captive by the Babylonians (remaining under):

> *"This is what the Lord says: see, I am setting before you the way of life and the way of death." Jeremiah 21:8*

Later we learn exactly what will come from these two groups. The Lord compares these two groups to that of two types of figs. The first group, the good figs, who chose to follow God into the captivity of the Babylonians in order that He may rescue them from their own sinfulness, leads to life. God outlines the plans He has for this group:

> *"My eyes will watch over them for their good, and I will bring them back to this land. I will build them up and not tear them down; I will plant them not uproot them. I will give them a heart to know me, that I am the Lord. They will be my people, and I will be their God, for they will return to me with all their heart." Jeremiah 24:6-7*

While this sounds like the sweet exchange, the alternate pathway leads to death. This was the pathway which was compared to the bad figs. In contrast to the good figs pathway, these were the figs that were too rotten to even be eaten (to be used for the intended purpose).

"I will deal with Zedekiah king of Judah, his officials and the survivors from Jerusalem whether they remain in this land or live in Egypt. I will make them abhorrent and an offense to all the kingdoms of the earth, a reproach, and a byword, an object of ridicule and cursing, wherever I banish them. I will send the sword, famine and plague against them until they are destroyed from the land I gave to them and their fathers." Jeremiah 24:8-10

It is your life, so you must choose your pathway. The consequences for choosing the path that patiently endures may seem like a hard one at first. However, the blessing we receive will far outweigh anything else in this world.

James gives a similar conclusion for the two pathways. The one in humble circumstances that perseveres receives the crown of life (James 1:12), while the one who is rich will pass away like a wild flower and he will fade away even while he still goes about his business (James 1:11).

I recently read a book, written by my favorite author who has helped me wade through many trials in my life. "If You Want to Walk on Water You Have to Get Out of the Boat," written by John Ortberg gave a quote that accurately describes this process of *remaining under*. He says, "If you can't get out of it, then get in," meaning, if the circumstances were put there by God, then get into it. What a frightening concept, but it is precisely why we need not worry about the trials of tomorrow. We face one at a time, realizing our life is out of our control, but the decisions we make to stay in the fight is ours.

This way of living, Paul and James assures us that we will be guided to living a life of *"Hope"* (Paul) and *"Completeness"* (James). Helps-Word Commentary tells us that the word *completeness* that James refers to is comparable to that of a pirate's scope. To use it to the full strength you must unfold it in stages until it reaches the *capacity effectiveness*. So, how do you become one of those people that God can use to your *capacity effectiveness*? James says it's through our trials that bring us perseverance that leads to maturity and finally completeness.

Paul tells us that suffering produces character traits that been proven genuine. It has been put to the fire and has been proven to withstand. Earlier, when we learned about the materials we use to build our foundations (1 Corinthians, chapter 3), we were warned that our character will be tested. Did you build with the *living stone* or kindling? Jesus compares this to rock and sinking sand in the book of Matthew. The people that hear His words and put them into practice are the type that build on rock that is left unaffected by the storms, high waters, and winds. The other type builds on sand, and when the storms came, the foundation washed away (Matthew 7:24-27). Is God in the midst of building your genuineness of character?

While these two verses lead us to the same perseverance that leads to hope and completeness, they start with two terms that vary slightly in their meaning. James is talking about trials, times when we are being tested. Maybe it is financially or with marriage. These are the times when we are called to make the hardest decisions we have ever had to make. For Shane's grandmother, who had to encourage her husband of 68 years to leave her to go to heaven, her character was tested. Through her faith in God that she would be alright, her character has never been so complete.

On the other hand, Paul is speaking about suffering, meaning distress, persecution, and affliction. My interpretation of this is *"facing your biggest nightmare."* Explaining to your children that you have to move because the unexpected events of the economy have taken everything you have worked for your whole life. Waking up to a call in the middle of the night to learn your husband died from a sudden heart attack at a young age. Perhaps, it means answering the door to a military commander explaining to you that your son won't be returning home from overseas. It could mean learning of your loved one's decision to end their own life. Or maybe it looks like leaving your house one beautiful May morning and innocently killing someone when you felt like you were doing everything right.

These nightmares happen every second of every day to people all around the world.

We fear to go through these situations, and yet we are told that the temples will be greater on the other side if we allow God to lead us through. I can't explain why some of us have harder lives or why there is another trial around every corner for some of us, while others walk through this world with little pain and devastation. This is one of those questions I plan on asking one of these days, but for now, I realize how much greater of a person I am for what I have been through.

I realize every day that I am not entirely complete, nor will ever be this side of heaven. What I do acknowledge is that I don't live for just myself anymore. I hate the fact that the man I hit had to die that day, but I don't get to decide when people get to die. That is Gods decision. What I get to decide is that instead of living in denial, I will live for this man. I will live a bigger, better (more fully devoted to God) life for him.

May 9th, is a powerful day for me. While other days of the year I still struggle handing my whole will over to God, on May 9th, it is a day that I don't live for me. I live for someone else, which means I'm 100% Gods. I find myself doing and saying things that I would never have the courage to do otherwise. I feel more complete than I have ever felt on that day. I love deeper, speak bolder, and see more clearly than any other day of the year. My goal is to live that way every day of the year. Perhaps my bigger goal is to live entirely for Jesus in the way, every day of the year.

We all have a chance to live for someone else. If we accept the cost that Jesus paid for all of us, we can live for Him. We do the hard things because we won't live for ourselves, but for the One who gave it all for us. The Apostle Paul lived a life of dedication in this way. I imagine that Paul understood the depths of his sin and how much grace God gave him for his sin against the disciples. This understanding drove him to a whole new level of appreciation for the love that God had for him. Written in Romans, by Paul we find that Christ died for all sin, but the life He lives is for

God. Paul continues to write to show us how this should apply to us:

> *"In the same way, count yourselves dead to sin but alive to God in Christ Jesus."* Romans 6:11

Again, several chapters later, Paul is still showing us his dedication to this way of thinking:

> *"For to me, to live is Christ and to die is gain."* Philippians 1:21

You may be in the midst of the fire. You may feel swallowed by the heartbreak. You may tell yourself that whatever trial, tragedy or sin you are facing seems too big to overcome. Challenge yourself to stop living for yourself, and it will change your whole perspective on life. Remind yourself every morning that everything you are doing in your day is done because Christ could not. He died for you, so you must live. In your mind, you may have convinced yourself that you don't deserve a more meaningful life, but the fact is that Christ does. This mentality builds a strong foundation in Christ. The people that live this life are capable of more love and sacrifice for others.

Paul not only wrote about this attitude, but he lived it out for all of us to see. For example, the book of Ephesians is written by Paul while Paul was in prison. What we expect to see is a bunch of complaining in the book of Ephesians. Let's just be honest here. If I wrote a book while imprisoned, it would be one sad and pathetic story. Yet we see Paul writing the contrary to what is human nature. Paul writes to the people of Ephesus in his jail cell to encourage them. He tells the people that he prays for them with thanksgiving and that God may be with them all. He is capable of more love because he lives for Christ, and his walk is all the evidence we need to believe it.

I should mention a word of caution here. When our foundations become stronger and impactful, it often means someone or something must lose ground in our life. There is an opposing force that loses ground as the glory is reflected brightly from our lives.

We may naively expect a team cheering us on. We are likely to find more haters than anything. People may become threatened by your life when you are devoted to God in unearthly ways. The opposition will come from the most unlikely places and relationships, but we must just continue to keep looking toward the light. Love the people who don't understand, because one day they might.

For some reason, I am always caught off guard and surprised when people come at me with a lack of understanding of my heart. I am always shocked when people misunderstand me to the point of assuming lies about me, and honestly, I am always horrified to see people persecute me for my love of God. But then, I am reminded of the Apostle Paul's warning that this will happen.

> *"Put on the full armor of God so that you can take your stand against the devil's schemes. For our struggle is not against flesh and blood, but against the rulers, against the authorities, against the powers of this dark world and*

against the spiritual forces of evil in the heavenly realms." Ephesians 6:12-13

There was a time in my life that I had no idea what this verse was referring to, but as God brought me to the trial in my life that was developing the character in me that he needed the spiritual attacks began. The power that God has in my life from that fateful day in May has been a threat to the dark forces of this world, and I find myself often putting the armor of God on as Paul instructs. The truth remains that God saved me when Satan tried to take me down.

Spiritual attacks have been a wakeup call to the truth of the forces against us. I have had to cling to my story with both arms. For some reason, the world would love to strip my story of God's redemptive love away from me. There have been attempts by people (even other Christians) to try and belittle my story. They want me to doubt what God has done in my life. They want me to make light of my dedication to God because of this situation. They want it to be a dim memory that I eventually *forge*" about. They want me to push all the blame off and live a life of denial because it just is *too deep*. At times, these people will shake me, but then God reminds me that this is my story. Just as He gave the Israelites a story to tell, that we are still telling to this day, He gave me a story. He gave me a purpose beyond myself to live, and I will stand against anyone who tries to rob that from me. He reminds me of the beauty of my mess when it touches someone else who is broken or hurting. For them and God, I will never let anyone rob me, so I put on my armor.

God is working in each of us as He builds our character into beautiful temples. While some of us may not appear as beautiful and unscathed as we wish, we must realize that beauty goes way deeper than the world wants us to believe. In Solomon's day, the temple's beauty was symbolic of the power of its gods. Solomon wanted the world to know that his God was the one true God, not to be even comparable to any other false god the people had imagined up. He thought the gold and precious metals that adorned the temple would be symbolic of the majesty of his God.

This makes sense, right? But, for the exiles that rebuilt the temple, they didn't have the resources Solomon had. What they had was enough, though, and its true worth was far greater than what Solomon had. The same applies to you and me. As we pick up the pieces of our lives, we may not feel like we have much, but what we do have is exactly what we need. The rebuilding of our Temple will be greater than ever before.

As I write this, the Museum from September 11, 2001, is getting ready to open. It lies where the old twin towers once stood. Now, we recognize not the majestic building of two huge buildings, but a smaller building that contains memories of the lives that were lost sacrificed and heroically saved that day. There is more glory there than ever before. This smaller building is more meaningful than ever. Pictures fill the museum of random people who were once of no importance to the world, but now signifying heroism and sacrificial love. As the visitors to the museum read story after story of the precious lives lost, I believe they walk out of the museum changed. Tragedy turns to a brilliant spark that changes people. Hearts walk out of that museum with a renewed sense of meaning. The world becomes a better place from the tragedy and heartbreak that unfolded on September 11, 2001. How great is our God!

CHAPTER TEN

WAIT AND WATCH

Did God Leave Us?

It was a summer like any for a family in Salt Lake City. They did their annual family reunion at Bear Lake hidden in the mountains outside of the Salt Lake area. For some reason, though, this summer took a tragic turn. Through a string of events, a mother and daughter from that family drowned trying to save one of the cousins. The mother that drowned was my sister's college friend. Watching the horror of everyone finding out and dealing with the tragedy reminded me of the harsh realities of this world. The funeral is over. Jeni and her daughter are laid to rest, wrapped in each other arms. The world returns to a new normal for all the family and friends. A journey of healing laid out before them just waiting for them to wander through the dark wilderness to a day when the sunshine returns.   The question that remains, is will the sunshine return?

By far the hardest part of going through anything tough is the waiting. It test's our faith and our hope each day as we wait on the healing. I am always shocked at the ache in my soul the weeks and months after losing a loved one. There's nothing to do in that time, but to wait for the heartache to ease. We may have worked through the healing process by placing God on our altar, building a foundation of faith and then realizing our character is stronger than ever, but that doesn't necessarily mean that the blessing of healing is right there waiting for us. We walk a path that is unknown to us, never knowing what God has laid out before us. That doesn't mean that as soon as we want the next thing to come along, it will be right there. Sometimes, what God leads us into is seasons of waiting. Sometimes that season is a day, sometimes a month and sometimes years. The Israelites, while in Babylon waited on God for 70 years.

In Jeremiah's letter to the exiles, he tells them that God has promised to bring them back to the Promised Land. He tells this to the discouraged, disheartened, and beaten down captives who have just lost everything. These people are facing 70 years in captivity, and yet the Lord gives them these words to hang onto:

> *"For I know the plans I have for you, declares the Lord, plans to prosper you and not to harm you, plans to give you hope and a future"*
> *Jeremiah 29:11*

Can you imagine being held captive in a foreign land, witnessing the burning of your temple, the death of loved ones, and now you will be a slave, and God tells you that His plans are for you to prosper, for hope and a future? He tells the people that they have no idea what He can do and that their life will be better than it has ever been because of the relationship that they will have with Him, but... they have to wait. This is the promise they have to hang on to.

God promised them that He would restore their fortunes and prosperity (Jeremiah 32:42; 44). Do we have a promise to hang on to as well? Absolutely. Paul has already told us we are God's temples. Don't you know that? We were built by God to be exactly as He created, and the work that He has prepared for us to do is already laid out. You were made for a purpose, and the purpose has already been created.

> *"For we are God's workmanship, created in Christ Jesus to do good works, which God prepared in advance for us to do" Ephesians 2:10*

There's the promise. You may be reading this; weary and beaten down from trials in your life, but this is your promise. You were never an accident. The events that have led you to where you are at were exactly what needed to happen to get where you are today. In the nine years since my accident, I have seen several instances where I have been able to help someone because I understood their grief. I've been able to share my story with people and have it touch their lives as well. The man that I hit, although he passed away, his life is still speaking today as I tell our story and share the love of God with people that couldn't imagine that the two could ever go together. If our story reaches one heart, then maybe all the pain we went through was worth it.

We are called to shine like stars in the universe (Philippians 2:15). Stars could never shine if they didn't have a fierce fire. It is the fierce fire that shines brightly for the rest of the universe to see. Within my weak body is a fire that is impossible to put out until my last breath on this earth. There are days that I have to be reminded of my fire, but anytime I tell my story it's fire renews.

How do we focus on being useful to God during seasons of waiting? Paul tells us that those who cleanse themselves from sin, made holy are those that are useful to God and are prepared to do good work. If you don't know what that looks like today for you, try finding the righteousness, faith, love and peace in your life. For me, in seasons of waiting, I normally read so many books that I lose track of what I have read. God leads me from one book to the next. It brings me joy, but I normally have to be intentional about setting time aside to do this.

Paul also suggests to surround yourself with people of pure hearts in tough times to get spurred on towards the right path (2 Timothy 2:20-22). This can be a dramatic shift of people in your life, but you will recognize the difference in your life rather quickly. Sometimes, God calls us to be leaders, sometimes advocates, sometimes followers and sometimes just friends. Be careful not to miss a season of just being a friend. The friends you surround yourself with during this time will fill your love tank up to prepare your heart for the next task at hand. Never overlook how God uses the people in your life to build you up, just as He used the Prophets Haggai and Zechariah to motivate and encourage Zerubbabel.

Now I know we live in a society that is anything but patient, but patiently enduring is the key. James compares this time to that of what a farmer experiences. A farmer that is impatient will never be successful. After planting the seeds, he must wait for the rains before he yields a valuable crop. He is likely to stress over all the unknown factors. A new farmer will worry over all the details, while an experienced farmer will know that there is nothing he can do that will speed up the growing season. He does his best during the period of waiting and hopes for the best, but he doesn't know the exact outcome of every season. He must wait. James tells us that we have to be the same. We have to be patient, and here's the kicker…we have to stand firm. He reminds us that we are blessed when we persevere under trials, and the Lord is full of compassion and mercy (James 5:7-11). Be patient, stand firm, be blessed as you wait and remember who God is. In a nutshell, it's how to get through seasons of waiting, according to James.

The year after my accident was the hardest year of my life. Every day seemed to be a struggle. Seven months after my accident when all my friends expected me to be over it (because they were), we went to a bowl game in down town San Antonio. I was excited to go and watch the game but hadn't realized what it was going to require getting there and back. After the game, we struggled through the crowd into the dark night sky where the mass numbers of people were in jams everywhere trying to get out of the parking lot. Because of my frugalness, we had parked a good bit away to get the best parking deal. We had to cross several busy intersections to get back to the parking lot. Horns honking, tires squealing, people yelling and mass amounts of chaos ensued. There were policemen directing traffic and ensuring pedestrians made it across the street safely, but it still seemed like chaos. Crossing the street in the dark, seeing headlights coming towards me just about sent me into a full-on panic attack. I could visualize my head shattering the windshield of passing vehicles. I felt completely out of control when I couldn't visually see all our friends. I was just so worried they would be hit by a car. I didn't want any of them to die. It terrified me. By the time we made it back, I was a wreck. I felt like I could hardly breathe. Embarrassed and humiliated by my reaction, I could tell our friends had no idea what to think when we reached our car.

I can remember getting home that night, extremely embarrassed by my reaction and ashamed that it had been seven months and I still had work to be done. I was eager for God to bring me the next thing. Waiting to be free was killing me. However, it was that night I understood that He knew my heart better than I and that I wasn't ready to just move on. My agitation of the *waiting* season changed into gratitude that God hadn't forced me to move on. I learned to be patient and to do the things that put me closest to him. I learned that I had to work on his timeline and not my own or anyone else's in my life. What I have discovered is that in these time periods, God's grace and mercy are abundant and He normally leads us to do the things that bring us the most joy as we heal. I decided that I would spend time doing something that I truly loved as I began my master's degree in Wildlife Science, a subject of passion for me. This time of learning and quietness was more healing to me than anything I could have imagined. After moving three years after my accident, God led me to a church and a month after I was done with my degree He called me to fill the position of the women's pastor, who was leaving shortly after.

To be honest, as I write this I am in another season of waiting. It is painful. I want to be so busy that I don't have to focus on the reality of what goes on in my life. As I write this, I find that there is nothing that brings more peace and contentment to my heart. It's right where God wants me until He calls for the next thing (that has already been prepared long ago for the day that my heart is ready). This waiting season is different from the last one. I know something now that I didn't know in the last season. I know the importance of working on God's timeline and giving Him the time and space to mend my heart. It is your faith that will build during these periods as you discover that God is always with you even if you don't fully understand His work.

For the exiles, the temple was built. They celebrated and were excited for what they had done amidst the turmoil with the encouragement and motivation of the prophets Haggai and Zechariah. There is a piece to the puzzle though that is still left out. Zechariah tells the people of a King that will come to save them:

> *"Rejoice greatly, O Daughter of Zion! Shout, Daughter of Jerusalem! See, your King comes to you, righteous and having salvation, gentle and riding on a donkey, on a colt, the foal of a donkey…He will proclaim peace to the nations. His rule will extend from sea to sea and from the River to the ends of the earth. As for you, because of the blood of my covenant with you, I will free your prisoners from the waterless pit." Zechariah 9:9-11*

We know what king it is that comes riding a donkey. The King of the World is Jesus. He speaks of a kind of king that changes everything. A king that is entirely different from any other king that has ever been. This king will be so humble that He will ride a donkey instead of resembling a king of those days recognizable by their arrogance on their war-horse.

This king would be like no other, and He would bring something unimaginable to that day.

Haggai tells the people that God has said:

"I will shake all nations and the desired of all nations will come, and I will fill this house with glory" Haggai 2:7

Jesus was what the nations desired. The glory (not the image) will be greater than Solomon's temple. As Haggai is saying this, I'm sure the Israelites were encouraged to know that even though their temple didn't look like much, Haggai promised something even greater. They had no idea what huge thing that God was going to do. He was going to send His Son, who would choose to die on the cross. Blameless and righteous, He would bestow a gift that would translate into filling every temple (believer) with the gift of the Spirit on the day of Pentecost.

They could never have imagined what He was going to do. I wonder if they waited every day for this great thing to come and save them. Were they discouraged each night when nothing came? Because you see, life went on for them too. After they built the temple, trouble still came. About 80 years later, Ezra returns to Jerusalem with a group of exiles to only find struggle, sin, and trouble. The Kings are still receiving letters from those who oppose God's chosen people trying to cause problems with them and stall any improvements they have made in Jerusalem. It was over 400 years later that Jesus makes his appearance. The humble King, riding the donkey that died and filled the temple came four *hundred* years later. They had no idea exactly how awesome of a gift was coming. Until then, the generations of people waited.

CHAPTER ELEVEN

CELEBRATE THE VICTORY

Remember the Temple

Celebrate. If there is one lesson we notice about the Jews, perhaps it could be that they celebrated. They may have been sinners who continually fell to their selfish desires, but they recognized a victory, and they celebrated it. What happens when we follow God with our whole heart, mind, and soul? We can't even fathom the great rewards that await us in heaven, as we recognize we must wait. The question we must answer today, is there reason to celebrate?

This story that witnesses such a great love and the rebuilding of the temple is found in the book of Ezra. I have wondered why the leader, Zerubbabel never had a chapter named after him. Wouldn't it be great to read what he, Zerubbabel had to say about this time in our history? Who was Zerubbabel? Was he a great leader who inspired his people or was it all God?

I believe we see the character of Zerubbabel through the prophet Zechariah. We get to witness the way God speaks to Zerubbabel through the Bible. God tells us three things here. First, He instructs Zerubbabel that it will be through God's Spirit that the Jews will accomplish the rebuilding of the temple. Second, they are assured that there will be mountains of troubles, but not to lose heart because these mountains will become flat land under the leadership of Zerubbabel. And last, God wants us to know that when the temple is finished under the hands of Zerubbabel, the people will celebrate and they will know that the words of the Lord through Zechariah were true.

If the rebuilding of the temple was a cake walk, would anyone ever question how powerful and mighty God is? Through Zerubbabel's leadership, moving mountains in the face of opposition, the people would sit back in awe that God could protect their paths to build the temple. I can only imagine how much

Zerubbabel celebrated at the completion of the temple. For a mere man, this had to have been a miracle as he witnessed what God can do.

Sometimes we forget to celebrate because it just seems like a bunch of *small things*, like *just* building an altar or *just* laying a foundation. Some days, *just* finding the strength to get out of bed may seem like it's all you can do. In the big picture, small things feel so insignificant. Why would we celebrate getting out of bed?

The Israelites celebrated those small things as they recognized that it took a power much greater than what they had to accomplish those small things. We may convince ourselves that those were not even comparable to our small things, but Zechariah reassures us of the opposite:

"Who despises the day of small things? Men will rejoice when they see the plumb line in the hand of Zerubbabel." Zechariah 4:10

The rebuilding of the temple took 22 years. That means that most days were filled with the mundane tasks that seemed like they didn't matter. It wasn't as if in one day they built the altar, and then the next they laid the foundation and then before they knew it...poof! There was the temple. No, what it meant was that most days were filled with the tedious jobs of doing the small things. Can you imagine building a house for 22 years, how mundane and insignificant that would seem after a while, and then 22 years later you stand in awe as you look at a house that stands before you.

This morning on the news, a story was aired of a 44-year-old American man who was climbing the Himalayan Mountains in Nepal, and fell into a crevasse, 70 feet down. Despite his broken ribs, broken arm dislocated shoulders, and internal bleeding, he managed to spend the next six hours climbing up to the top using his ice axe. He was so badly injured, he had to slowly inch his way up until he made it to the top. Once to the top, though, he had another three-hour crawl back to his camp where he endured frigid temperatures until the following morning when rescuers were finally able to reach him. He doubted each inch he crawled, and as he completed one obstacle to only find the next one, he kept going. Each little inch he crawled must have seemed so insignificant, but the next morning, lying alive in a hospital bed, he must have been grateful for each. Without enduring the first inch, he would be lying in the bottom of that crevasse still. His success shows that *he* is a person that chose to celebrate the small victories instead of looking at the overwhelming task ahead.

Do we want to struggle through the *small* things? No, but in the big picture, they aren't small things after all. So, we celebrate them. One at a time, we celebrate.

Looking back at my recovery, I would have thought choosing forgiveness was just a small thing, but little did I know the huge leap I took that day. I wish I would have celebrated that moment more because, without it, I would still be suffocating. Handing over to God my fears, one at a time seemed so insignificant, but without each of them, I would never have found the freedom I live in today. I wish I would have celebrated them more.

A way of worshipping God for me today is by celebrating. When my daughter brings home a good report card, we celebrate it. When my husband gets a promotion at work, we celebrate it. When one of us has had a good day, we celebrate it. When we finish a challenge, we celebrate it. We don't need a grand party or an award to go on the wall, but we stop and thank God for what *He* has done in our life. May 9th is a day of celebration for me. My human nature wants to climb into a hole and hide on that day, but my love for what God has taken me through makes me celebrate it. My goal on that day is to do something I wouldn't normally do to recognize my thankfulness. Every year this looks a little different but has ranged from going camping, to running a Spartan race, to making a nice dinner to standing up against a man who continually picked on weaker people. All this as an offering to God for what He has done. Confidence to stand up is always a Holy celebration.

On a side note, you will recognize your Godly friends here because they will celebrate with you. A friend of mine who celebrates beautifully is a dear friend who lost her son. She celebrates his life probably one way or another every day of her life. She celebrates him when she sees dragon flies and lilies that remind her of him. She celebrates at his grave by decorating it with the seasonal decorations. She runs marathons and obstacle races and hangs the medals at his grave. She talks about him and thanks God for him every day. She chooses to be blessed by having him for a short while instead of asking God why He would do this. She chooses to celebrate. We recently just ran a race, and she wore a shirt with a picture on the front that showed her reason for running. As we ran, we were both reminding ourselves that we were doing it because not everyone can…and so we chose to celebrate.

If you can take what has shaken your world and turn it into passion and into a love that far exceeds any motivation of this world you will witness Gods hand as it so tenderly sits upon your shoulder. This is when

God speaks through your life. Instead of just a Sunday church attending Christian, you become a fully devoted follower of Christ.

For the leader of the exiles, Zerubbabel, he became more than just a halfhearted follower. God's approval of all the work that Zerubbabel put into the temple can't be missed when you read this verse:

"I will take you, my servant Zerubbabel son of Shealtiel, declares the Lord, and I will make you like my signet ring, for I have chosen you, declares the Lord Almighty." Haggai 2:23

A signet ring was a ring that was inscribed with a letter or insignia that indicated by whose authority or ownership one was dictating. This was comparable to the notary stamp that we see on our important documents of today. This stamp normally indicates which person of the authorizing state has the authority to approve the record. Until it is stamped, it is worthless. Esther writes of letters being sealed by the King's signet ring, which was sealed with softened wax and the impression of the King's signet ring placed for the recipient to know that it was legitimate. God is telling Zerubbabel that he will become like God's own special ring, showing that he was chosen by God, for a specific purpose and has been designated with authority. Zerubbabel, through his faith in God, would be able to leave a mark on people. He would be able to influence those around him. He was chosen.

If Zerubbabel had walked away burned out and disgruntled, he would have given no glory to God. As the leader of these exiles, he chose to celebrate. As the altar was built and they began their celebration, they laid their humble sacrifices upon the altar. Their faithfulness was no doubt surprising to the doubters around them. I'm sure people wondered how, after 70 years of captivity, and after only building an altar they could celebrate. What redeeming love do you have to hold to be able to celebrate in such a way? Is there any better way to be a shining star in this universe than that? The celebration is contagious. Everyone wants to be part of a good thing. Unfortunately, very few will walk through the storm to get to the celebration with you.

This latest season of waiting has been a tough time for me, but there was a turning point in which I recognized that I had gotten off course a bit. My husband had just got a big promotion at work which dedicated him to the last enlisted force rank tier in the military. It was a big promotion for him, and we were thrilled despite the hardships that it had taken to get there. We threw an open house for people to come by and celebrate this achievement with us. After the second, less than enthusiastic, *fulfilling their obligation* type of friends had left the house, I realized we had surrounded ourselves with non-celebrators. I still love this group of people, but there is nothing more depressing than not being able to celebrate. Surround yourself with people who are celebrating the victories with you.

Not everyone is willing to celebrate on May 9th with me either. I knew I had a huge problem with a spiritual leader when he encouraged me several years ago, on May 9th to *just forget about it*. I was in the midst of a celebration that day, looking for ways to bless people in my life when he dropped that ball in the middle of a lunch meeting. I recognized at that moment that there was no way to respect his spiritual insight if he couldn't recognize what God had done in my life. I choose to remember, and so I celebrate. My celebration is my worship for God, and it doesn't resemble a big party or bash, but that of looking outside of myself to be able to love someone else a fraction of the way God has loved me. This joy will never be robbed from me on this earth because amid the battle there wasn't one person who could rescue me.

Does my life look like a bunch of mountains that Zerubbabel faced? Maybe, only God knows. Can He flatten them out before me to make my pathways clear? Absolutely. Will it be day after day of a bunch of small trials? Most likely. So, I ask myself, am I as lucky as Zerubbabel to be God's "signet ring"? What about you? Are you God's signet ring, or perhaps this was simply a promise to Zerubbabel in that exact situation and circumstances. To answer that question, we go to where we started. We skip to the New

Testament and read again what Paul says about the temple:

> *"Do you not know that your body is a temple of the Holy Spirit, who is in you, whom you have received from God? You are not your own; you were bought with a price. Therefore honor God with your body." 1 Corinthians 6:18-20*

You are precious to God. He recognizes the laboring work every day you face to get where you are. He understands the hardships you endure and the victories you have accomplished. He sees the struggles you face. He paid the ultimate price for *you* and wants *you* to be His signet ring, the holy temple of the Holy Spirit. He gave His dearly beloved Son for *you*, even while you were in exile.

Our celebrations influence those around us. They can witness the all graceful God through us and our walk. Ultimately, they can be a signet ring because of our journey. I can only imagine the people that we influence wearing a stamp, but can I fully grasp what that means? Can I truly understand that there is nothing more loving we can give each other than our stories to light up the pathway to God? That they may wear a stamp showing authority and become a child of God because of our loving guidance along the way is overwhelming.

If we could do a time warp to have a conversation with the Jews of the Old Testament and we could talk about God, we would likely hear them talk about the temple. Their faith, their hope and their commitment to God all started at the temple. So, if it was so ingrained in the Christian faith in the Old Testament, how is it then that most of us don't even know the story of the temple? When did it become less important? The people of those days couldn't forget about how important the temple is, particularly due to the hardship, the sin, the enduring persecution that they endured to build it. They would remember the journey that took generations to accomplish from escaping slavery in Egypt to finally having their own temple. They likely remembered the promises that God made to Abraham and Moses. They remembered the temple.

It is with the same emotions that are stirred within us as we celebrate Memorial Day and the 4th of July. We remember the wars, the lives that were lost to make our country what it is today, and suddenly we are filled with a renewed sense of love and appreciation.

If you can genuinely relate to the road of the Jews, whether through the trials and tragedies you have faced, or whether you have experienced the redeeming love of God, you must remember your temple. *The true tragedy occurs when we throw out the story that led us into the sweet embrace of a God that longs for our hearts.*

Remember the temple.

AUTHOR'S NOTE

Gratitude and heart-felt emotion arise as I tell this story. To a man that I don't know, but whose story is forever entangled with mine, I hope to know you one day. I hope to share the story that his life brought to mine and the legacy I leave because of him. It is my prayer that his name and his heart never leaves mine and will be on my lips until my last dying breaths. My hope is that he is embraced by the physical loving embrace of Jesus as I am by the Holy Spirit's and that one day we will be of the same. There are no words that can accurately describe the way I feel for such an unknown person. How can I love someone so deeply, yet know nothing of his story? It is the mark of the binding love that Christ brings. This is the love that changes the world.

Shane, Charleigh, and later Tanner were the gifts that gave, and continue to give me strength to take the steps out of my own anguish. For me, they are evidence of God's mighty hand in my life and are exactly what I need every day to find the strength to follow Him. How do I know that God exists? They are my evidence on a daily basis. I distinctly remember days sitting in our small living room in San Antonio, rocking our newborn baby and just knowing she was a gift and that there was indeed a Creator. She was the gift too great to have ever given me.

I must admit that this book was written with no intention for anyone to ever read it. I figured that perhaps it would be a great way for my kids to understand this period in my life. Somewhere along the way, I had some near and dear people that encouraged me to look beyond and see what God truly had intentioned for me. Considering, I was reading through the old testament one day when the whole story line came together in a sweet whisper of redemption that led to a mad frenzy of typing for the next year, this book has been a tender gift to me.

Realizing that my story is not too far different from the Israelites has been amazing. I have never really understood this immense portion of the Bible until reading it that day. The story came alive, and I realized that in God's mercy, he made sure we understand that we are not alone in building our temples. He knows that we feel like exiles while here on this earth. His gift is to make sure we know, we are ***Dearly Loved Exiles***.

ABOUT JANELL MELLISH

Janell is a veteran of the United States Air Force, in which she was a Training Instructor in Basic Military Training, and in Security Forces. She earned her Master's Degree in Natural Resources from Texas A&M University in College Station, Texas.

Janell's military training led her to a passion for coaching people to realize their potential and ultimately their "Champion." She currently runs a women's boxing gym in Cheyenne, Wyoming and